Best wishes

Jean Cirb

The
Good Ole Days

Collected Columns By Jesse Culp

Mountaintop Press

Published by

Mountaintop Press

Division of Culp Associates, Inc.

P. O. Box 698
Albertville, Alabama 35950

Library of Congress Catalog Card Number: 88-92503
ISBN 0-929835-00-X

Printed in the United States of America

FOREWORD

This book is a response to requests which have come for many years from readers of my columns, listeners to radio and television programs and folks I have rubbed shoulders with through the years in appearances at storytelling festivals, business and civic club meetings and community get-togethers. I am grateful for their interest in having these bits of Americana preserved.

It is also an expression of my personal conviction that the customs, ideals, ideas and everyday living practices which are such a rich part of our heritage need to be preserved and kept for present and future generations. I trust that these vignettes will contribute interestingly and meaningfully to such a treasury.

Most of my stories stem at least in part from my own experiences and recollections, albeit with occasional embellishment. But many have been brought to mind by others who have shared their own experiences and observations, including fellow storytellers, writers and speakers. Thus, these writings are truly the work of many.

My heartfelt hope is that this book will inform, enlighten and entertain. And that it will help to preserve some of the threads from the fabric of our past.

Jesse Culp

PREFACE

Jesse Culp's columns have aptly depicted an important part of our American heritage and are down to earth accounts of how folks lived during the Depression years and the decades that followed. He has shared his "Good Ole Days" stories and reminiscences in numerous storytelling festivals, business and civic clubs and community gatherings.

As with Joel Chandler Harris' Uncle Remus, customs and wisdom are woven into Jesse's descriptive tales. These usually have one theme such as possum hunting, egg gathering, the one room schoolhouse and the country store.

A masterful storyteller, Jesse — in his recounting possum hunting, for example — starts the reader off on a chilly night "after the first bit of fall has arrived and the moon is as big and round as a pumpkin." He goes on the hunt with a couple of skinny, bony blue tick hounds and a burlap bag. Down at the pasture swamp near a big old persimmon tree he finds his possum, "glowing beady eyes, scowling face and that toothy grin." The tale ends with the possum being cooked and served with a batch of sweet potatoes.

Surprisingly, in Jesse's country store ramblings, he sees clearly the similarity between the supermarket of today and the old country store. Both stock many different items in comparison to the specialty shops. In the center of the country store was the pot bellied stove where the latest gossip would be exchanged by the men and the world's problems thrashed out. Nothing has replaced the pot bellied stove. The similarity stops there.

In writing of the Depression Jesse reminisces: "It was a time when people had very little money to spend. We grew our own food, made things that we needed, and did without most everything else." He goes on to say that "out of this kind of life came a spirit of neighborliness which has been pretty much lost in our modern days."

As the son of a high school principal in a small town, I can identify well with Jesse Culp's recall of the past. Despite our massive airports, Gallerias, interstate limited access highways, and cities with their glitz and glamour, most of us mourn the disappearance of a family-oriented locally centralized way of life. Jesse's stories richly embellish our heritage.

Bill Nichols
Member of Congress
Washington, D.C.

The "Tin Lizzie"

Few things have ever come along in this country that changed our way of life as much as what happened October 1, 1908.

That was the date Henry Ford introduced his Model T, the little car which came to be affectionately called the "Tin Lizzie."

The Model T literally put this nation on wheels. And things have never been the same since! When the Model T came along, it brought revolutionary changes in the daily lives and habits of individuals and families to an extent difficult for people to imagine today.

It was extremely hard for men who had driven horses and buggies all their lives to adapt to the changes that were necessary to drive these "horseless carriages."

For example, all their lives they had been in the habit of just hollering "whoa!" when they wanted to stop. Now, they had to learn to take one foot off the gas pedal (or push up the gas lever) and put the other foot on the brake pedal when they wanted to stop.

Maybe that sounds easy or even automatic to the average person today. But it sure wasn't an easy habit to change for someone who had handled a horse all his life.

One of the first things most proud owners would do when they bought their first car was to build a shed to house it in. And, in many cases, one of the first things they did after that was to drive into the shed and holler "whoa!" instead of putting on the brakes, thus driving right through the back end of their new car shed.

Another habit that was hard to break was that of always driving up to a hitching post or tree so as to be able to tie one's steed before leaving it for awhile.

In the early days after most folks got automobiles, about the only change in appearance in country churchyards on Sunday was that the cars were parked in front of the trees, right where they had always tied their horses. It took a long time for those car owners to break the habit of insisting on parking in front of a tree.

Well, there is no doubt about it! The Model T brought revolutionary changes to our American way of life.

And I'll always have a special affection for this little black car which was as tough and stubborn as a mule. But it could get us to where we were going at breakneck speeds of up to 20 miles an hour. If we could hold it in the road.

Cranking A Model T

If you've ever tried to start your car on a cold day, only to find the battery dead or too weak to turn the engine, you know how frustrating this can be. But you don't know what such trouble really is unless you've had to crank an old Model T on a cold winter morning.

As Model T buffs know, all the early Model T's had no starter on them at all. You started them with a crank, which was engaged to the crankshaft through an opening in the bottom of the radiator housing.

The first ones had the crank permanently mounted on the bottom of the radiator, where it just dangled there all the time. But later models had a removable crank which was kept under the front seat of the car, to be inserted into the slot when cranking time came.

It took a mighty lot of elbow grease applied to the crank to turn the cantankerous little engine over enough to crank it. That was especially true on a real cold morning, when it seemed like the entire car would roll over before the engine would turn.

It was a treacherous task too. Just as you managed to give it a good hefty turn of the crank, the engine would fly back the other way, causing the crank to kick back at you. If you weren't quick to get out of the way, it could break an arm or leg.

Finally, in the 1920s, Ford started putting starters on their Model T's, or least offering them as an option.

Soon the "self starter" (as it was first called) became a standard item. But the hand crank continued to be a standard item too, because it had to be used about half the time, and practically all the time in cold weather.

Back then, folks were accustomed to the dangers of getting kicked by mules. So it didn't seem too strange to them to get kicked by Model T's when they tried to crank them.

One way that Model T owners tried to avoid this was by parking their car right at the top of a steep hill on cold nights, so that they could easily push the car off to crank it rather than have to risk injury to life and limb by turning that bodacious crank!

Some ingenious Model T owners even rigged up an incline with two greased poles so they could push their car down this and give it a fast running start to crank it.

I could write an entire book about the ingenious things people thought up in order to operate their Model T's and keep them running. And I might just do that, when the Ford people decide to start making 'em again!

Shade Tree Mechanics
And Barbers

Driving down a country road the other day, I saw a fellow out under a shade tree with the front end of his car jacked up and he was obviously busy trying to perform a repair job. It reminded me of the "shade tree mechanics" who were familiar characters back in the days when I was growing up.

It started back in the Model T days, when most car owners worked on their own cars. It wasn't so hard in those days, because with a pair of pliers, a monkey wrench, some bailing wire and a good dose of common sense you could fix just about anything that could go wrong with a little black "tin lizzie."

Today's complicated and expensive automobiles are a different story. But we still use the term "shade tree mechanic" to refer to an amateur or a pseudo-professional mechanic who is in reality mostly just a tinkerer — oftentimes with disastrous results.

Now, without necessarily drawing a parallel between the two, let me ask how many of you remember the "shade tree barbers" of the good ole days.

When I was growing up in the country during the Depression days, every community had one or more barbers who did most of the hair cutting for the men in the community. They were not full-time professional barbers. They were farmers or laborers who cut hair "on the side" on weekends and at night.

Their barber chair was concocted by turning one cane-bottom straight chair upside down on the front porch or out under a shade tree in the yard and setting another chair upright on top of it.

6

Their tools were a pair of hand-operated clippers, scissors, comb and brush. A clean white flour sack or guano sack was draped over the shoulders of the "victim." And when the haircut was finished, the sideburns were shaved with a straight razor whetted on a big black leather strop.

Finally, the excess hair clippings were brushed off the neck and ears and a generous quantity of talcum powder was applied.

You climbed down off the teetering perch, handed the man a dime, and you were fixed up for another month insofar as your hairstyle was concerned.

Why, I can still remember the very first haircut I ever got in a genuine cityfied barbershop. I was a grown boy at the time!

This is a far cry from today's modern barber shops with their sophisticated vacuum-powered equipment, and certainly from the hair stylists which many men patronize.

Most young people today never heard of what we used to call a "bowl haircut." That was just what the name describes: it was a deal where a bowl was turned down over your head and all the hair was cut around the bottom of the bowl. I'm sure thankful that has gone out of style!

Oh well, "shade tree barbers" have gone out of style, and "shade tree mechanics" are fast going too.

For many of us, however, they're gone but not forgotten. Once you've had a haircut in a cane-bottom chair with a pair of dull clippers on a sweltering summer day with those tiny clipped hairs sticking to your sweaty neck, you'll never forget it!

Weather Sayins'

With the coming of fall and the approach of winter every year, I like to dig out my collection of old-timey weather sayings and review them once again.

It seems that every time I talk about old weather signs, it strikes a familiar cord with many folks.

Here are a few I have collected through the years:

When leaves show their undersides or back during a breeze, rain is likely.

A heavy dew in the early morning is a fair weather sign.

When you see lightning in the north, rain is likely within 24 hours.

When distant sounds or whistles appear louder, rain is likely.

When visibility is extremely good during humid periods, and when trees on distant hills are easily seen, rain is likely.

Rising smoke is a fair weather sign, but when you see smoke going downward or showing very little rise, rain is likely.

Birds perch more just before a storm because the low barometric pressure makes it more difficult for them to fly. When you see birds flying unusually high, it is a fair weather sign.

When tree frogs croak, look out for rain.

Hens or barnyard fowl pick at themselves, "oiling their feathers," just preceding rain.

A good sign of the approach of damp weather is the aggravation of corns, bunions, or arthritis pains.

When air bubbles increase in a goldfish bowl, stormy weather is approaching.

In winter seasons, sycamore trees with shiny spider webs sparkling indicate that cold weather is coming.

When you see a rainbow in the morning, this indicates there will be a shower by noon.

Dense fog at dawn is a sign of clearing skies by mid-morning.

Strong southerly winds indicate rain within 24 hours, while northerly winds are a sign of dry weather ahead.

The absence of birds around water denotes an approaching storm.

White fluffy small clouds are a sign of fair weather ahead.

Odors become easier to detect just before a rain. High pressure usually traps odors like a lid due to air density, while lowering pressure releases odors.

Many old weather signs are surprisingly accurate because they are based on several generations of "down-to-earth" people who have observed cyclical changes in the weather.

Today, meteorologists can watch the weather patterns unfold and move all over the earth through the eyes of satellites in orbit hundreds of miles above us. And we in turn can see much of what they are seeing on the radar screens on television.

But there's still a lot to be said for the folk wisdom of our ancestors, who watched weather patterns for generations rather than just hours or days, and handed their conclusions down from one generation to the next in the form of our colorful (and often accurate) ole timey weather signs!

Weather Signs

Okay, all you weather buffs! It's time to review some of the old weather signs and see if we can guesstimate what sort of winter we'll have.

The first thing you need to do is to count the number of fogs that we have during August. That's the way we determine how many snows to expect the coming winter. It's an old weather sign: for every fog in August there'll be a snow the following winter.

Another old saying regarding snow is that — during wintertime — when your fireplace is going and the wood makes a peculiar popping sound like someone walking in crunchy snow, you can figure that snow is likely to fall soon.

Hunters suspect that a hard winter is in prospect when they begin to notice that rabbits, squirrels and foxes have unusually thick coats in the fall of the year. And farmers look for the thickness of shucks on corn at harvest time. If the corn has unusually thick shucks, look out for a cold winter ahead.

Many old weather signs predict the approach of rain. For example, the old folks say that the hooting of an owl in the daytime, the hollering of raincrows, and ducks flapping their wings on land as if they were in the water — all these things are an indication that it will rain soon.

Turkey buzzards that are flying when heavy clouds are approaching almost invariably head toward and over the approaching clouds if they are rain clouds. And house flies tend to collect and to stick and bother much more just before a rain.

You can look at spider webs early in the morning and tell whether it is likely to rain that day or not. If the

webs are short and well braced with cross webs, rain is indicated. If they are long and loosely braced, fair weather is likely that day.

Weather does tend to run in cycles and follow certain patterns, and farmers and outdoorsmen have been able to predict with sometimes amazing accuracy what the weather is going to do.

And so:

When the sky is red in the morning . . . and there's a rainbow before noon . . . and the stars are ghostly dim and dull . . . and a ring forms 'round the moon . . . when the crows caw long and loudly . . . and the flies stick tight and bite . . . when fish jump out of the water . . . and sounds travel far at night . . . when you can't get salt from the shaker . . . and your corns give you extra pain. . . you don't have to consult the almanac . . . you just know it's going to rain!

Our Ways of Talkin'

One of my favorite things about our country is the way we talk.

I wouldn't change it for anything, and I hope those good old words and phrases which have come up through the backwoods trails will never disappear from our lingo.

One thing that we country folks appreciate is good "vittles." Like "turnip sallit" (cooked with fatback) and "hoppin' john."

After a fellow "tanks up" on that kind of "vittles" he's about ready to lie down on a "pallet" and get some "shut eye." And such eating will cause "a-body" to "fleshen up" and feel "right pert."

Everybody knows that what some folks call a sack is really a "poke," and that you "tote" things in it. Too much of this will soon get you "plumb tuckered out" or just plain "white eyed." And those first days of hard plowing in the spring will leave you "stove up" for a "spell."

You probably won't find in medical texts the right terms for describing your health either. You may be feeling "po'ly," "tolerable" or just "fair to middlin'."

Many of our words and phrases are fascinatingly colorful and descriptive. "Catty cornered" is diagonal, and "spittin' image" is an exact copy.

When you get hemmed in on both sides in a matter you are caught between "a rock and a hard place," and that's when you're liable to get flustered or "in a tizzie."

Even mild-mannered folks sometimes get a "hankerin" to use some strong language on occasions, and some — rather than cuss — have invented some borderline expressions like "plague take it" or "dad burn it."

13

And when we're indebted to someone we're just plain "beholden" to them.

If something's over there, we say, "It's over yonder."

Rather than pry an object loose we "prize" it loose.

We enjoy indulging in a few mispronounciations which have become colloquialisms — such as "kivvers" for covers, "toreckly" for directly (meaning soon), and "hope" for help.

When a girl is unusually "purty" we describe her as "cute as a 'speckled pup'."

And when something is unusually hard to come by, we say it's as "scarce as hen's teeth."

If someone "asts" you if you'd like a "cheer," you think of just pulling up a "cheer" and settin' a spell. "Peart" means you're feeling well, like "peart as a young heifer."

"Purt-near" means pretty near or just about. And on the other hand, a long distance is "a fur piece."

"Rat cheer" means right near, as in "lay it rat cheer."

"Auto" has nothing to do with a gas-guzzler. It means "should," as in "I auto go to work."

Well, I'm obliged to stop for now, because I've plum run out of space!

How Do You Spell It?

They just don't make dictionaries like they used to! Have you noticed that? When I'm writing, I run into all sorts of problems because I can't find a dictionary that has lots of words in it that I'm all time using. So, I can't find the correct or official spelling of them.

For instance, there's the work "larrapin." Everybody knows that means something that's super delicious, or lip-smackin' good. As in, "man, that stuff tastes larrapin good!"

Then there's "rench." You know, like when you wash your clothes and then rench them.

And how about "keered?" Back in the good ole days, when a fellow loved a girl he really "keered for her."

Take "shet" for instance. When we younguns' were growing up we were always taught to be modest and speak only when spoken to around our elders. Children were often reminded that "nothing looks better on a youngun' than a shet mouth!"

In the spring, when the weather started warming up, it was not uncommon to get stung by a wawst. Best I can tell, my dictionary spells the same thing "wasp."

I've looked everywhere in dictionaries and can't find "wheewhonkered" or "whompeyjawed." These are common words for things that are crooked. A structure that doesn't stand up straight is, of course, "anti-godlin."

Back in those days folks used language that was more descriptive and understandable than our modern vernacular. Like "hawg meat," "tooth dentist," "ground peas" (for peanuts) and "widow woman." In fact, there were two different kinds of "widow women." A "grass widow" was one who had divorced her'n and a "sod widow" was one who had buried her'n.

15

We had windows back in those days. But we called them "winders" or "winder lights."

That was before cholesterol or viruses had been invented. So we just et all the hen aigs we wanted. And when we got sick, it was generally "pneumony fever," "gallopin' consumption," "epozudick" or plain old "croup."

We ate arshtaters and sot on cheers. Dinner was around noon and supper was about sundown. And when we had eaten all we wanted, we had had a "bait."

Folks were always real friendly and neighborly, never failing to invite you to come to see them. "You'uns come," they'd say (later shortened to "y'all come"). Or "foot my door sill," "come in and set a spell" or "come and take some vittles with us!"

See what I mean? I reckon we've just sort of fell down on our spelling and grammar and everything. Ever since we got shed of the Blue Back Speller!

Blue Back Spellers

As I sit here typing this column on my electric typewriter, I'm thinking about how things have changed since the days when my mother and daddy went to school — learning to spell with the old Blue Back Speller and working out their arithmetic with chalk on a slate.

How many of you have ever seen a Blue Back Speller? This was a little paperback book that was the standard in schools in those days. It was used to teach spelling phonetically, and I continue to be amazed as I think of how effective it was. My mother attended public school through the equivalent of the third grade, and she could still out-spell me by the time I got to high school!

I can remember that we still had her old dog-eared Blue Back Speller when I was growing up. It was kept — along with other relics — in our old family trunk. But somehow, it was discarded and lost. Now, I'd give anything if I still had it as a keepsake.

And how many of you remember the little slates that students used to carry to school to work their lessons on? This was before the days of paper tablets, and I can also remember my mother's old slate which she saved for many years.

Back in those days, every student had a slate, which was like a miniature blackboard with a wood frame. Lessons were worked on it with chalk, and then erased with a rag.

Those were the days when students went to school in small one-teacher schools near home, and where the teacher would have students recite their lessons in the classroom — one grade at a time.

Times were much less complicated then, and it was rare for young people to go through high school—much less graduate from college!

The schools literally concentrated just on reading, writing and arithmetic. And when youngsters learned those basics they dropped out of school and started making a living for themselves and their families. The remainder of their learning was gained in the school of hard knocks.

Young people (and we older folks too) need much more formal education to make it in today's more complicated world. But we all still need a heap of our ancestors' good ole common sense too!

One Teacher Schools

One of the victims of progress in public education is the one-teacher school. And as I look back on some of its good points, I wonder if we have lost something in the demise of the one teacher school that we never have been able to regain in public education.

My first five years in school were spent in a one teacher school with about 20 pupils. It was named Culp School, because just about everybody who went to school there was a Culp or close kin to us.

I learned my three Rs from some of my own teaching kinfolks, and I never had any better teachers, from there all the way through college.

The school was about a mile from our home, and of course, I walked every day. This was quite an adventure, too, because there was a little branch of water which ran under a little bridge across the dirt road. And I generally took time to catch a few tadpoles or minnows, rig up a flutter mill, or chunk rocks into the water.

The school building itself was a single room with a big pot bellied stove right in the middle, in which there was always a roaring fire on cold winter days.

In those days it was a common practice for women teachers who were not married to "board" in a home in the community. The teacher was generally about the most "looked up to" person in the community, and it was considered quite an honor to have her stay in one's home, as well as a special asset to the children in that home, who had the advantage of being with her a lot of extra time.

While the school was under the jurisdiction of the county board of education, it was — for all practical purposes — really managed by the local school trustees, who were honored and respected in the community. I can't ever remember a time when a teacher was "called on the carpet" by a parent or the trustees for disciplining an unruly child. In fact, the trustees and parents as a whole firmly backed the teacher in this regard. It was a standing rule at our house that if we got a whipping at school, we could expect one twice as hard when we got home!

Each fall, before time for school to start, the men of the community would have a "working" at the school, to clean the grounds, make needed repairs, and cut plenty of firewood for the coming winter.

Because of changing population trends and changing patterns in public education, one teacher schools were closed in great numbers in the late thirties and early forties, a trend which was accelerated in the fifties.

Certainly we have gained many fine things in facilities and teaching techniques in consolidating schools. But we have lost some of the closeness and interest between teachers, students and parents which were so valuable to all in the one teacher school.

Box Suppers

How many of you have ever been to a box supper? Box suppers used to be a popular thing but I seldom hear of one any more.

It was traditional for just about every community to have a box supper at the schoolhouse every year. And while the main purpose of the annual box supper was to raise money for the school, it was one of the social occasions of the year.

The girls would each fix up a box full of food and decorate it real pretty and put their name on it. These boxes would then be auctioned off, and the highest bidder for each box would get to eat the food with the girl who brought it.

Every boy who had a favorite girl friend started saving up his money weeks ahead of time, so he could have enough — hopefully — to buy his girl's box. In fact, it was sure a miserable happenstance for him if someboy else, especially a rival, outbid him!

Sometimes, just for meanness, some of the boys would get together and form a conspiracy against another boy, especially one who was love-struck with a particular girl. They would keep running up the bidding to make him have to pay a high price to get to eat supper with his true love.

In some cases, this would get out of hand, tempers would flare, and even fights would ensue. But mostly, it was all a fun thing.

Sometimes the older women brought boxes too. But usually their role was to bake cakes for the cake walk, another popular event at the box supper.

And there was the traditional country store, where everything from handcrafts and baked goods to fresh parched peanuts could be bought at a bargain.

Now, folks have generally turned to less "down to earth" forms of socializing. And raising money for the school takes on a more commercial air.

But despite the more sophisticated school systems and the radical changes in community life, the one fact of most schools having to scrape and scratch to get enough money to operate on doesn't ever seem to change.

Maybe the educators need to take another look at ole timey box suppers for solving education's perennial money woes. They might not come up to taxes as revenue producers, but they sure are more fun!

Possum Huntin'

When there's a clear chilly night after the first bit of fall has arrived and the moon is as big and round as a pumpkin, every country boy knows it's time to go possum huntin'.

Some supposedly educated folks may try to tell you that this little native North American animal I'm talking about is correctly called an oppossum. But, of course, you and I both know that he's just a plain ole possum.

Anyhow, getting back to our possum hunt: We'll need an old kerosene lantern, a good strong flashlight, a sharp double bit ax, a strong burlap sack without any holes in it, and a couple of skinny and bony blue tick hounds.

It's not too hard to find the possums. They'll be down in the pasture swamp right near that big old persimmon (more properly called 'simmon) tree that has a good crop of golden yellow ripe persimmons on it.

So, right after supper, when it's good and dark except for the big yellow moon, we'll get the dogs and head out.

Pretty soon Ole Blue will start yodeling and Ole Rip will come 'a-running to join in, and we'll know they're on the trail of old mister possum. By the time we get to them, they'll have him up a tree.

Both dogs will be clawing at the tree and jumping as high as they can, looking up at their prey. We'll shine the flashlight up and catch his glowing beady eyes, then get a look at his scowling face and that fierce toothy grin.

Whoever feels up to it will climb up the tree apiece, at least far enough up so's he can shake it good and hard. With a little luck, he'll jar that possum loose, and he'll fall right into that open burlap sack being held underneath.

If that doesn't work, we'll just have to send the sack up the tree and grab the possum in it. Or, if it's a little tree, we'll chop it down with our trusty ax.

Well, after repeating this a few times we'll head for home with a sackful of sulling possums. We'll shut them up in the crib and fatten them a few days on plenty of shelled corn and other goodies.

Then, we'll be ready to cook them with a batch of new crop sweet potatoes, and have us a real feast!

Dinner Bells

In our modern society we have all sorts of emergency warning and communication systems which people can use to summon help when needed — such as the 911 telephone setup in many cities and communities, early warning systems for bad weather and other emergencies, rescue squads and other organizations and institutions.

And of course, this country has long had a national emergency warning system incorporated around our radio and television stations.

What did folks do back before we had television and radio — and even telephones — in most rural areas? Well, they still had ways of sending out calls for help.

One of the key instruments in those days was the dinner bell.

Every rural family had a dinner bell, and of course each dinner bell had its own particular tone. Everyone in earshot could tell whose dinner bell was being rung, not only by the direction from which the sound came but because of the tone of the bell itself.

Around dinner time every day in our community there was a dinner bell concert, as dozens of bells would start ringing at practically the same time to call in the hands from the fields.

But at any other time of the day, the frantic ringing of a dinner bell was a distress signal. It meant that somebody's house was on fire, someone had been kicked by a mule or had had some other kind of accident or there was an emergency of some sort.

When such a sound rang out across our hills and hollows, everybody dropped what they were doing and came running ! That was our version of the hospital call of "stat," meaning "come quickly!"

Now and then there was a family too poor to even own a dinner bell. So they simply hung an old worn-out plow point from a tree limb with a piece of baling wire and banged on it with a hammer or piece of pipe.

Another distress signal was the rapid firing of a shotgun into the air. And if all else failed, somebody would get on top of the barn and holler as loud as his lungs would allow!

Those ways of emergency communications seem crude by today's standards. But folks found ways to make do with what they had to do with — even in the matter of helping each other. And to paraphrase one TV character: "It worked for us!"

Ole Timey Telephones

It was on March 7, 1876 that Alexander Graham Bell patented the telephone. And things haven't been the same since!

How many times have you talked on the telephone this week? And how many times did your phone ring when you wished it wouldn't — like when you were right on the edge of your seat watching the climax of a mystery on TV, and it was somebody calling the wrong number, or else they just hung up when you answered!

The telephone is a mighty important factor in our daily lives. Recently I saw a demonstration of an instrument which enables one to see as well as hear the party on the other end of the line. It reminded me of how times have changed since the days of our community telephone systems.

Every home had an old crank telephone hanging on the kitchen wall, and each family had its own ring — so many longs and so many shorts. But that didn't matter too much, because just about everybody who was in hearing distance of their telephone stopped what they were doing and picked up their receiver to listen every time the phone rang to see what was being said.

When it got so we couldn't get our kinfolks on the phone we knew right away that the line was down somewhere between us and them, so we'd start following the lines until we found the break and patch it back together.

In places the line was mounted on poles, but in others it was simply attached to an insulator nailed to a convenient roadside tree.

And every boy in the community seemed to delight in sharpening his shooting abilities with his slingshot by shooting at the telephone line insulators.

Our phone system was connected to the outside world by a line which was hooked on with "central" eight miles away. Everybody knew "central" not by name but by voice and title.

"Central" was a friendly lady who had the telephone switchboard in her house. And it worked just like it did in Mayberry: when you wanted to call somebody you just picked up the receiver and told "central" who you wanted.

She knew more about everybody's business than did their preacher and banker put together!

The modern telephone systems of today have contributed much to progress. In fact, the wheels of business and society would nearly grind to a halt if we had to suddenly revert back to "central" and the precarious phone lines of the good ole days.

But it is a part of Americana that many of us will never forget!

Communications

Seems like every year there is a proliferation of new gadgets designed to save us time, labor and energy —to make our lives more comfortable, enjoyable, entertaining and fulfilling.

The space age has brought literally a technology explosion, and all of a sudden we have products in our hands and surrounding our lives that I couldn't have dreamed of just a few years ago!

I can look around a typical business office today and see numerous gadgets and pieces of equipment which simply boggle my mind.

A busy executive punches a button and his telephone automatically dials (almost instantaneously) any one of dozens of frequently-called numbers which he has programmed into it. And if it's long distance, his phone talks to the phone company's computer, and not another human gets involved until someone picks up the receiver on the other end — perhaps halfway around the country or around the world.

If the person on the other end is away from his office or his desk, his automatic answering device takes the call and records the message, ready to be played back to him automatically anytime he wants to call back to his own office from any telephone in the world.

He can call back to his home or office from his car or even from a jet airliner, zooming through the skies at 600 miles an hour seven miles above the earth.

And if he has some calculating to do, he slips a tiny computer the size of his credit card out of his wallet or shirt pocket and performs in minutes the arithmetic which a bevy of accountants might have slaved over for hours a generation ago.

I can remember when many columnists and journalists wrote their copy by hand, before even manual typewriters (much less electrics) were universally used in newspaper offices. Now, typewriters have become almost extinct in the newsroom, as reporters do their stories on computers, staring into a cathode tube that looks like a television set.

I'm about to get like the old codger at the country store who quipped to me recently: "Son, I don't believe hardly anything I hear any more, and only half of what I see!"

Computers

Remember when computers first came out? It took a huge room to hold one of the things, and they cost such a bodacious sum of money that only a government agency or a giant corporation could afford to buy and operate one.

I couldn't comprehend the things they could do —like perform hundreds of complicated calculations a minute.

Now, salesmen carry them around in small briefcases and housewives even use them to keep up with the inventories in their kitchen pantries.

Newspapers set type with them and elementary school children operate them just as casually as I used to work my arithmetic assignments with a pencil and tablet.

Some computers can now talk in human language, while others can understand spoken language and obey verbal commands.

Now, they have supercomputers. And these totally boggle my mind. Like what is called a class six supercomputer which is able to do 1.2 billion calculations per second — 50,000 times the ability of a personal computer!

Remember when small electronic calculators first came out? They were small enough to be held in your hand, but they cost several hundred dollars apiece.

Now, they're the size of credit cards, run off of solar energy and not only compute but they tell time, wake you up in the morning, operate a perpetual calendar and perform numerous other functions.

I was talking the other day with a friend of mine who is a watch and clock collector. "Wrist watches are obsolete now," he said. "What we now have is computers that we wear on our wrists. And some are getting so cheap that we don't think of repairing them when they stop working; we just toss them in the garbage," he added.

Recently I took my car in to the shop to have some work done on it and the mechanic started explaining to me about the various computer systems built into the car and how they operate. He lost me somewhere between the brake pedal and the radiator!

And the fellow who owns the dealership kept me company while my car was being worked on by moaning about how he had spent $600,000 for new computerized diagnostic equipment just a few months ago, and now some of it is already obsolete.

I'm about ready to head for the old creek bank with a fishing pole. But then, there's no use to do that. The creek is clogged up with silt and beer cans, and the water is too contaminated for fish to live in.

Life seems to be getting more tejius all the time!

Space Age Marvels

A television commercial shows a husband arriving home early from work, reading the instructions his "career woman" wife has left for supper preparation.

In one effortless motion, he takes a chicken out of the freezer, pops it into a microwave oven, hits an automatic defrost button, and presto! Minutes later his wifemate arrives home, they remove the fully cooked chicken from the oven and the family's dinner is ready.

Even allowing for the discrepancy between television and real life, the scenario is still a little farfetched. Yet, it isn't too different from reality these days to be believable.

My, how times have changed since those good ole days of cooking with the old Home Comfort wood-burning stove!

It was one of my regular jobs after school to bring in stovewood and keep the big woodbox replenished with dry stovewood to feed the old range, which could burn up several armloads of wood cooking a single meal.

And for my mother, cooking supper was a task that required several hours of hard work, slaving over that hot stove.

Compare this with the microwave oven, which cooks food quietly and quickly without conventional heat, using radio waves to excite the molecules in the food itself and causing them to heat up the food and cook it with their own agitation.

Sixty years ago, if someone had tried to tell my daddy that a cook stove like this would someday be used, he would have gladly signed the papers to commit them to the crazy house!

How could you explain to a good honest, sincere, hard-working fellow out in the woods cutting stovewood that one of these days folks would calmly push a button and:

Cook a slice of bacon completely done in a minute, on a piece of paper towel, with the oven not even getting warm?

Bring a cup of water to a rolling boil in a couple of minutes, without the handle of the cup even getting warm?

Warm a slice of apple pie with a dip of ice cream on top of it without melting the ice cream?

Cook a big roast well done in less than 30 minutes?

Frankly, it's hard for me to believe such things myself, even though they are commonplace these days right in my kitchen!

Admittedly, I'm the same guy who didn't really believe them when they started talking about sending men to the moon. And when I sat in my living room watching those astronauts walk around up there on the moon's surface, I still had trouble believing what I was seeing and hearing.

However, many of us are doing things almost as amazing in and around our own homes and places of business every day in this space age. And never giving it a second thought!

Home Comfort Stoves

Back in the good ole days, a fixture in everybody's kitchen was the Home Comfort Range. And I can still taste those big biscuits and all the other goodies that my mother used to bake in that big cook stove, which is completely foreign to today's generations.

For those who never saw a Home Comfort Range, it was a grand old cook stove made of heavy cast iron that could eat up an armload of stovewood in a hurry. But it was a truly great cooking instrument!

It had a spacious oven that would bake a fat pone of cornbread to perfection, make a cake fit for visiting preachers, and turn out a mouth-watering blackberry pie.

The cook served as her own thermostat. A hot oven meant stuffing the firebox a little more frequently with stovewood, while a slow oven meant letting the fire die down to hot glowing coals.

Across the entire top of the range was a little enclosed cabinet with an enameled front — the warming closet. This was where you put food that you wanted to keep warm until serving.

Hanging off the end of the range next to the firebox was a big water tank known as a reservoir. This was where you kept the hot water you needed for bathing, washing dishes, etc. (Nobody ever head of such a thing as a hot water heater). It had a big door on top, and when you wanted hot water you opened the door and dipped out the water you needed with a kitchen boiler. Maybe this was why the water in the reservoir always had a slight greasy film on top!

I'll never forget how hungry I always was when I got in from school every afternoon. The first stop was

always the warming closet, where I could count on finding such goodies as a baked sweet potato or leftover sausage and biscuits.

However, the truly wondrous moments came when —running into the kitchen from the long walk from a mile away, where the school bus stopped — I spied a big clean white flour sack spread out in the middle of our big kitchen table. This always meant that Mother had baked up a big batch of teacakes or gingerbread.

On the days when this happened, I somehow didn't mind so much having to tote all those armloads of stovewood in and pile it up high in the woodbox behind that big Home Comfort Range.

With the modern conveniences we now have in our kitchens, it would be a terrible burden to have to go back to cooking on an old Home Comfort Range. But I hope we will preserve some of these grand old relics in our homes or museums.

It would be a shame for future generations never to see or know of the grand old cast iron lady which warmed our kitchens and satisfied our hunger in the good ole days — when the family kitchen instead of the neighborhood drive-in was the gathering place for refreshment, fun and fellowship!

Sunday Dinner

As we all grow older, we individually have a storehouse of favorite memories from our childhood days. And I think that Sunday dinners hold a lot of memories for most of us because they were really special occasions back in the good ole days.

Sunday dinner is still kind of special for most families, but not in quite the same way as it used to be when many of us were growing up.

I can remember that when I was a boy there was seldom a Sunday that at least one other family failed to come home with us from church to "take dinner" with us. Often it was the preacher and his family, because our church was on a circuit and the preacher lived in a distant community. So every Sunday it was standard procedure (or at least on "preaching Sundays") for somebody to invite the preacher to take dinner with them. For sure, if the preacher was there to eat with us, we could figure on having fried chicken for Sunday dinner.

It didn't seem to matter who or how many came home with us to eat, my mother had plenty of food for everybody. In fact, most of it was prepared after we got home from church.

One of the first things was for one of us kids, or Daddy, to go out in the yard and catch two or three chickens and wring their necks and dress them, while somebody else was getting a fire built in the stove.

After awhile, all the food was cooked and spread, and it was time for the grown folks to gather around to eat.

It was the custom in those days for the younguns to wait and eat at the "second table," which meant that the elders got all the choice pickins' of the food. After they got through eating (and sometimes lingered around the table talking for awhile), they got up and went to sit out on the porch or around the fire to talk some more. Then we children were called in from play and the table was set for us.

I was nearly grown before I knew that a chicken had anything but wings and a back! In fact, till this very day those are still favorite pieces of the chicken with me.

Yes, Sunday dinner was quite a special occasion in those good ole days But I'm thankful that today we no longer make the children wait to eat while the older folks go first. This custom was well intended, as a mark of respect for the elders. It has now, however, been replaced with more thoughtful customs regarding children.

Anyway, most of us who are old enough to remember have fond memories about those special Sunday dinners of days gone by!

Poke And Potlikker

I can hardly wait for spring to arrive every year! Warm days with more sunshine, the scent of fresh-turned earth, pretty flowers in bloom and the calling of the whippoorwills in the woods. All these and countless other things make springtime truly special.

After a long hard winter, my country bones get powerful hungry for some fresh poke sallit, turnip greens and potlikker!

Now, in case some of you city slickers don't know what poke sallit is, it is a delectable dish made from poke, or poke weed, which grows wild around southern climes.

Poke, or poke sallit (as most of us country folks call it), is a tall coarse perennial herb with a smooth stem that ranges in color from green to purplish. It has large simple leaves, and in the summer it produces clusters of small greenish flowers and eventually dark purple berries. Different folks spell it different ways. But however you choose to spell it, poke is mighty fine eating. The leaves, that is.

One of my favorite country cooks has an old family recipe for preparing poke sallit that goes back for several generations in her family.

She cleans the poke by washing it in three waters, then puts it in a large boiler with plenty of water to cover it and lets it boil for about 20 minutes. Then she drains all the water out, covers with clean water, then presses all the water out again. This is important to remove toxic juices from the poke leaves.

Meanwhile, she has another boiler with a good-sized piece of fatback or white meat boiling in it. She places the poke in this and lets it continue to boil until it is done and tender. Some bacon drippings may be added for extra flavor.

Needless to say, you eat it with a big pone of hot cornbread and lots of fresh buttermilk or sweet milk.

Well, as much as I love poke sallit, I'll have to confess that there's one thing that I like to eat even better. That is a big pot of spring turnip greens with lots of potlikker and a big, thick pone of cornbread.

Of all the things to eat ever discovered, I do believe that turnip green broth soaked in cornbread crumbs is the very best. Why, I'd take it over a T-bone steak any day! The next best thing I know of to eat, after turnip greens, potlikker and poke, is that same pone of cornbread crumbled up in a big tall glass of cold milk. Then comes such other good eating as homemade ice cream, steaks and such.

There may be lots of things we country boys are ignorant about. But good eating isn't one of them!

Fireplace Cooking

One of the interesting things going on in our society today is a re-discovery by the current generation of some of the good things about the good ole days. Like cooking over a bed of hot coals in the fireplace.

That's the way families used to do all their cooking. In fact, cook stoves are a relatively new invention for homes, particularly in rural areas.

Though this had given way to the old Home Comfort wood burning stove by the time I was born, the kitchen fireplace in our house still bore the marks of cooking utensils used there during my daddy's growing-up days. And we still enjoyed baking sweet potatoes in the hot coals in the fireplace on a winter night.

Recently I was in a hardware store looking at the fireplace accessories, and noticed grates that had an attachment on the end where an iron cooking pot could be attached. "We are selling these attachments as fast as we can get them," the proprietor said, "because so many people are enjoying cooking in their fireplace these days."

One reader remembers how good the biscuits were that her mother used to cook on the hearth on cold winter nights. "They were better than any hot rolls," she recalls.

"Anyone who has never eaten sweet potatoes, light bread and biscuits cooked in a fireplace has sure missed a treat," she adds.

In addition to heating the home and providing the heat for cooking, fireplaces also helped to light the home in early days.

Abraham Lincoln is said to have spent many hours reading books by the light of a fireplace. And, as a matter of fact, I have done so myself.

By the time I was growing up, we had kerosene lamps to light our home, and even the more sophisticated Aladdin Lamp to read and study by. But it was still a special joy to lie down in front of a bright roaring fire in the fireplace on a cold winter night and read a favorite book.

Maybe the light was not the best for reading, but the atmosphere was mighty fine. And I wonder if the dim light caused much eyestrain anyway. Seems like fewer youngsters wore glasses then than do today.

At any rate, the fireplace was a center of attraction in every home in those days. As the major source of heat and light, it naturally attracted everybody in the house on cold days. Thus, it became the favorite spot for families to gather for fun and fellowship.

Fresh From The Garden

Everywhere I go during the spring and summer, I see folks busy working in their gardens. Those of us who grew up on the farm just had it bred in us to start working the soil, planting seed and growing food when springtime arrived each year. And I reckon that's something that never gets out of our blood.

Of course, as the summer wore on we really began to enjoy the fruits of our labors in the form of those wonderfully fresh vegetables which we harvested right out of our garden.

In those days, times were hard and it was a necessity for us to grow most of the things we ate. We simply couldn't afford to go to the store and buy them. But now, lots of folks who can afford to buy all their food at the grocery store still like to plant a garden every year for some very important reasons.

Families who have just started growing gardens have discovered how much better and fresher the vegetables are when they walk out to the garden and pick or pull or dig them up, then head straight for the kitchen and cook them. Shucks! We country folks grew up on that kind of goodness!

Something many people today have not yet discovered is how good lots of those vegetables are without even being cooked.

I used to come home from school in the spring of the year thinking I was on the brink of being starved to death. So, I'd head straight for the kitchen to find some warmed-over biscuits in the warming closet of the old Home Comfort range. Then, biscuits in hand, I'd head for the garden to pull some succulent green onion tops to go with my biscuits. That was sure 'nuff good eating!

45

Strawberries and ice cream are mighty good. But the best thing was to go right to the patch and pick those juicy red berries off the vine and eat them right on the spot, just wiping the dirt off on my britches leg.

Roasting ears pulled fresh off the stalk (better known as "roast-nyers") and boiled are mighty fine with lots of butter. But when you are hungry, they're mighty tasty when you walk out into the patch and pull a big ear of corn and gnaw it raw right off the cob. And so on with turnips and carrots and potatoes, and numerous other fresh vegetables from the garden.

Maybe that's one of the answers to conserving expensive energy these days. Maybe we're cooking things too much.

Hopefully, times won't get so bad that we'll have to revert back to some of the cruder ways of living which characterized daily living for us poor country folks back in the Depression days. But it might help some of us more than it would hurt us if we had to!

Neighborhood Grocers

Browsing through a big new supermarket the other day, I marveled at the wide aisles and the tremendous array of merchandise, all so carefully and systematically arranged by departments.

The computerized checkout lanes in some of today's food stores are a space-age marvel in themselves, as I realized when I watched the checkout lady zip my purchases across a gadget which electronically read the code printed on each package and recorded it — via an in-house computer — with brand name, package size and price information on my checkout slip.

It all set me to thinking, with some nostalgia, about the demise of the neighborhood grocery store and those friendly grocers who were so much a part of our lives in days gone by.

Those were the days when you always bought your groceries from your own neighborhood grocer, who provided services unheard of today. Such as home delivery. You placed your order with your grocer in the morning and it was delivered that afternoon.

Your grocer knew your likes and dislikes, and he always made sure to stock just the brand names and package sizes of things that you wanted.

He even knew your family eating habits. He knew what days of the week you always cooked a special dish. So, if you ordered it that morning early, he'd make sure you had it on your kitchen table before lunchtime.

If you wanted a special cut of meat, you just stood by the chopping block and showed him how you wanted it cut, all the while exchanging neighborhood gossip.

There was no such thing as a checkout lane. You just gathered up your items from over the store and took them one by one up to the cash register. And when you got through, he would ring them up for you. (Or, you might just walk in the store and hand him your shopping list, and he'd gather up all the items for you and then ring them up).

You didn't have to pay him right then. In fact, most folks bought their groceries on credit, and the grocer sent them a hand-written bill the first of the month.

Back in those days, grocery shopping was a social event as well as a family necessity. There was no such thing as grocery carts, frozen food cases, automatic door openers or electronic cash registers. More than likely, you would drop in to the grocery store just about every day — not only because you had to buy fresh foods on an almost-daily basis, but because you simply liked to visit with your friend, the neighborhood grocer.

Of course, none of us would choose to discard our modern supermarkets and go back to such a system of grocery shopping. But wouldn't it be nice if we could somehow enjoy the modern trappings of today's supermarkets with the friendly atmosphere of those old-fashioned neighborhood grocery stores!

Pot Bellied Stoves

Every fall of the year, when we begin to get a few chilly nights and mornings that remind us of the coming winter, I am reminded of the vast improvements that have been made in heating devices since I grew up back in the good ole days.

For instance, the pot bellied stove. The pot bellied stove is one of those significant items of Americana now disappearing from the scene, and I sort of hate to see it go!

Those of us who grew up in the good ole days know what an important fixture the big black pot bellied stove was in homes, churches, stores, schools and other public gathering places.

I'll never forget the big one in the country church where my family went, and how hot that monster used to get about preaching time on a cold winter Sunday night. Folks sitting on the front rows didn't have much trouble staying right in there with the preacher on his warnings about the fires of torment, as they began to shuck their coats and frantically wave their funeral home fans!

Sometimes in the one-room school I attended, the days would get so cold, with that wind whipping around the little frame building, that the teacher would gather us kids close to the big pot bellied stove in the center of the room to recite our lessons.

Through the years, there have been more world problems solved by men sitting on nail kegs around pot bellied stoves in country stores than in all the diplomatic conferences and world councils put together!

That big pot bellied stove in the country store centerpieced the very place to swap pocket knives, talk about the weather, discuss the state of the nation, catch up on the neighborhood gossip, and generally keep informed about the details of neighborly living.

Today our more modern and cleaner heating devices have just about replaced all the old pot bellied stoves, which are becoming about as extinct as wagon tongues, singletrees and guano horns.

They're not all gone, however. In fact, just the other day I walked into an ole timey country store. There was that old pot bellied stove in the middle of the store, just where it's been for almost 100 years.

Despite the high cost of energy, I don't think the pot bellied stove will make such a comeback as the fireplace has. But I'll always treasure my special store of memories about the life and times of gatherings around the old pot bellied stove!

Modern Kitchens

The other day I stopped by to visit with a friend of mine who runs an appliance store, and he was talking about some of my stories about pot bellied stoves, old Home Comfort wood burning ranges and other ole timey things in the home.

"Here, let me show you some of the new space age appliances which are out for today's modern kitchens," he said. And for the next little while he demonstrated some appliances right there in the store that boggled my mind.

"Do you believe I can lay this piece of paper on top of this stove eye, boil a pan of water on it and not burn or sear the paper?," he asked.

Well, I didn't believe it. So he laid a sheet of paper on top of the cooking eye, set a pan of cold water on it and turned the switch. In a few seconds I saw steam starting to rise from the water. And as it began to boil he lifted it off the stove, handed me the barely-warm piece of paper and invited me to put my hand on top of the stove eye — which was not too hot to touch. "Does it with electromagnetic waves," he explained in the midst of my puzzlement.

Then he showed me an oven which is a combined convection oven, microwave oven and conventional oven all wrapped in one — stainless steel and self-cleaning, of course.

Next to it was another type of cook stove with solid eyes that never need cleaning. "This little thing in the middle of each eye is a sensor which automatically regulates the heat," he explained. "If, for instance, you go off and forget something you're cooking, this sensor won't let it boil over," he added.

And on and on it went for awhile, by which time I was having to physically push my bulging eyes back into their sockets.

"Shucks, used to be that you could buy a fine house for $30,000," he said. "Now, you can easily pay that much just for your kitchen appliances," he continued, as he punched a few buttons on his solar-powered credit card-size calculator.

I knew there had to be some catch to all of this!

Lighterd

Fireplaces are making a big comeback these days, as more and more folks are re-discovering the joys and pleasures of sitting in front of an open fire on a cold winter evening, reading or watching television or fellowshipping with family and friends.

I can't imagine what sort of madness ever possessed home builders to cause them to start building houses without fireplaces anyway! But, whatever the circumstances, fireplaces are making a big comeback.

That has opened up a whole new economic ballgame for landowners who have hardwood timber which they can cut and sell for firewood. It has also brought on a big demand for kindling for use in lighting fires.

Every country person knows that the finest kindling is lighterd, which of course is fat heart pine that has had the resins in it hardened or "sugared" or crystalized over a long period of years.

Lighterd is commonly found in the form of pine knots or stumps which have laid in the woods for a long time, with the soft parts of the pine having rotted away, leaving just this "fat" heart section remaining.

Lighterd is getting pretty scarce now, but it used to abound in most woodlands when I was growing up, and everybody used lighterd splinters for starting fires.

Like most families, we always had a big lighterd pile, where we deposited the pine knots and stumps as we found them in the woods. When I was a boy, one of my regular jobs was to split splinters and keep them replenished in the lighterd box which always stood by the old Home Comfort stove in the kitchen and by each fireplace in the house.

Folks with fireplaces these days sometimes have a problem obtaining good kindling to start their fires with, unless they have one of these new-fangled gas starter jets which are now being installed in many fireplaces.

Fortunately, I have a good friend who has a wood-working shop who shares some of his wood scraps with me. That's the next best thing to pure lighterd for starting wood fires.

Now, if I can locate another good friend who has a big crop of peanuts all picked off and dried and who will share some of them with me, I'll be all set to sit by my fire this winter and eat parched peanuts and throw the hulls in the fire. That's really living!

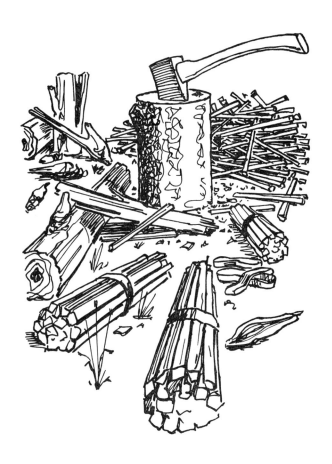

Coal Oil

A common fixture in every household a generation ago — and one which is now about as scarce as hen's teeth — is a can of coal oil. Some of you younger readers don't know what I'm talking about. But you'll recognize the product by its modern name, kerosene.

Yes, we used to call it coal oil, and we used it for a variety of important things around the house. For one thing, it was our fuel for lighting. In the days before electricity in farm homes (and some in the city) we lit our homes with kerosene lamps. One of my regular jobs was to fill the kerosene lamps, trim the wicks and wash the globes every few days, so we would have good light from our lamps.

We never had electricty in our home when I was growing up, so all the way through school I studied by an Aladdin lamp, which was the best light one could have from a kerosene lamp. It had a "mantle" which was some sort of flimsy substance which glowed in the heat and flame, emitting a bright light. But if the flame was turned up too high the "mantle" would catch fire, and blaze up like a brush fire!

In those days coal oil was a major item for sale at every service station or country store. It was kept in big barrels or drums with a hand pump on top, and folks just brought their kerosene cans and bought a gallon at a time, for five cents.

Up until a few years ago, it had gotten almost impossible to find kerosene for sale. However, with the growing popularity of kerosene heaters in recent years, many places are selling it once again.

Even aside from its use in kerosene heaters, many people have continued to use this unique petroleum product in many different ways. Some hunters use kerosene in their hunting lamps, kind of like we used when we hunted possums at night with our old kerosene lanterns.

Painters find kerosene useful to clean their brushes and cut the paint from their hands, and some mechanics use it for cleaning their tools and garage equipment, since it is not so flammable as other compounds. And of course some use it for heating their homes.

I often think of how coal oil has come up in the world, though, when I see a big jet airliner come humming over and realize that those mighty jet engines are powered by the same stuff that fuelled our old Aladdin lamp when I was a boy.

Isn't it interesting to see how things come and go, and how our use of and attitude toward certain things changes with the passing of time and the progress (or regression) of man?

A few generations ago, no prudent head of a household would let his coal oil can get empty. Now, few heads of households even have one, and most don't know what one is.

We're all dependent on electricity to light our homes. But when the power goes off we are almost helpless in the dark. Unless we have kept on hand an old lamp filled with kerosene with the wick trimmed and the globe cleaned and ready to light our way just like it used to back in the good ole days!

Solar Energy

Until recent years, we never heard folks talking much about energy. Everyone was somewhat aware of the fact that we all utilize various forms of energy and depend upon it constantly. But we always had plenty of sources of cheap energy which we pretty much took for granted.

However, in more recent times, as energy (such as gasoline and electricity) has become more and more expensive, we have begun to realize that we cannot take it for granted any longer.

The scientists and experts are constantly research-ing and searching for new sources of energy which we can harness and utilize. One of the sources is the greatest energy source which we have always had around us, and that is the sun. All sorts of devices have been invented and are being tried as a means of further utilizing the energy of the sun and harnessing it for many of our daily chores.

I've just been thinking about how we used to employ solar energy in so many ways which have almost faded from the scene in modern times.

One of the greatest ways was in food preservation. Those were the days before home freezers, or even steam pressure cookers. So we either canned our excess food in the summer, or we dried it.

Instead of freezing apples and peaches for later use, we peeled them, sliced them and spread them on a piece of tin roofing and let them dry in the sun. And my, what delicious pies they made the following winter!

We may have canned a few peas and beans, but mostly we just let them stay on the stalk until they dried in the sun, then we shelled them and stored them for winter use. They weren't as good as the fresh green ones during the summer gardening season, but they lacked little in taste and nutrition for our dinner table during the long days of winter. And about the only problem we had with them was just keeping the weevils out of them.

During the summer it wasn't even necessary to heat up the stove to warm our Saturday night bath water. We could draw that galvanized wash tub full of cool well water at dinner time and let it set in the hot sun all afternoon, and it would be just right for bathing in that night.

There certainly wasn't much sophisticated technology involved in any of this to be sure. But, as simple as it was, it worked well for us.

Maybe that's where we'll have to go back to in order to start utilizing the energy of the sun in these modern times. Back to some of those good ole timey ways!

Electricity

A nationwide survey has revealed that 34 percent of all Americans feel that electricity was the greatest invention of all times. The next closest thing was the wheel, at 11 percent.

I wasn't asked in that survey, but if I had been I would have certainly voted for electricity — hands down!

In a way, it is unfortunate that so many people today have never known what it is like to live without electricity. But I came along before the rural electric cooperatives were organized beginning with the creation of the Rural Electricification Administration in 1935. And I can tell you from personal experience that this has totally revolutionized daily living for folks in rural America!

We lived on a remote dirt road, and it just wasn't "cost effective" for a profit making utility to run an electric line to our place — until the co-op came along.

We lighted our home with kerosene lamps, cooked with a wood burning stove, drew our water from wells and springs, washed clothes around a big black washpot in the back yard, let the milk down to the cool water in the bottom of the well to keep it from souring in hot weather, and did without ice except for hauling an occasional block of that precious frozen water from the ice plant in town.

Maybe you're thinking from reading this that I'm talking about a long time ago. Well, I'll tell you that this was still happening on the Culp place until the mid-forties. And for lots of rural families, this way of life was standard until into the early fifties, when the co-ops finally got electricity to just about everyone in their service areas.

Now, thanks to the country's 1,000 rural electric cooperatives, 99 percent of all families in rural America have electricity — just as their city neighbors have had for as long as most can remember.

Pause for a few moments and try to count all the ways that electricity serves you in your home or workplace. I tried, and ran out of fingers and toes several times before I thought of all the ways electricity serves my family 24 hours a day!

A kilowatt hour of electricity, which costs just a few pennies, is far and away the biggest bargain I can think of. Sure, it costs a lot more than it used to. But when we think of all it does for us, it beats all other expenditures by a country mile!

I'm going to try to remember this when I get my next bodacious electric bill. Then I'll head for the refrigerator and get myself a cold drink!

The General Store

The other day I was rambling around in one of those bodacious big stores where they sell everything, and I got to thinking about how we're gradually getting back to the very same merchandising concept of the old fashioned country store of my boyhood days.

In those days the country store sold just about everything an average family would need. It was a gas station out front and a general store inside.

There was no such thing as a supermarket, as we know them today. You bought most of your food in cans or bottles or cases or crates. Big items like flour were sometimes purchased by the barrel.

And fresh food items were produced at home anyway, so there was no need for such a thing as a refrigerated produce or dairy counter. Which was a good thing, because such a thing hadn't been invented, so far as I know.

Sometimes you ate real special things right there in the store. Like sardines and crackers, or a big hunk of sharp cheese cut right off a big hoop of cheese, along with a nickel box of soda crackers.

And the pickle barrel was also a favorite place, where you reached down into the salty brine and fished out a big fat sour pickle to eat.

But food was only a small part of the offering at the country store. Toward the back there were shelves full of dry goods — print cloth, thread, pretty dresses for the ladies and girls and overalls and pants and shirts for the men and boys. There were shoes for every member of the family, all the way from brogans to work in to Sunday go-to-meeting dress-up shoes.

And in the very back of the store there was the hardware department, where you could buy everything from plow points to horse collars.

Right in the middle of the store, of course, was the familiar pot-bellied stove, in which was kept a roaring fire on cold winter days. This was the gathering place for the menfolks when it was too wet to plow, and here all the latest gossip was exchanged and all the world's problems were thrashed out.

Well, along came "progress," and specialization. The country store bit the dust, as we figured out how it was best to have different kinds of stores to sell different kinds of things.

Now, we're starting to discover again that it sure is convenient to be able to go into one store and buy everything you need right there. So, we're getting back to the general store concept again, but with some substantial wrinkles.

Why, this store I was in had nearly as much floor space as all the stores in the whole town had when I was growing up! There wasn't a pot-bellied stove to be found in the place, not a pickle barrel nor a hoop of cheese setting on a nail keg. And out front there was a big cement field nearly as big as our old home place.

There was quite a bit of gossiping going on, mainly among the salesgirls at their fancy cash registers at the checkout lanes. And they looked at me real funny when I asked them where I'd find the horseshoe nails!

Washdays

It's fun to reminisce about the good ole days. But, truthfully, the best part of it is that we can just preserve in our memories the pleasant things and conveniently ignore all the things that were so arduous and unpleasant about growing up in those times in the past.

Life is so much easier and more pleasant for us today, thanks in part to the numerous time-saving and labor-saving devices and conveniences which most of us now have at our command. And I can think of no better illustration of this than what has happened to change washing and drying of clothes from a terrible drudgery to a relatively inconsequential task.

For instance, cold winter days make washdays a headache for housewives who have to hang wet clothes on the line outdoors. But they are of no concern to increasing numbers of housewives, who wash and dry their clothes automatically by flipping switches right in the comfort of their homes. Of all the modern conveniences of this age, automatic washers and dryers have perhaps done more to liberate women from backbreaking toil than anything else.

Going back a generation or two ago, washday was a full day of toil, not just for one woman but for several people, and that usually meant the man of the house and all the children too pitching in to help.

We had quite a rig for washing clothes at our house. In fact, it was an entire complex known as the washhouse. There was a huge wash pot mounted in a homemade rock furnace, complete with a big chimney. This was housed under a tin shed, which also covered the long wide shelves on which the big galvanized wash tubs sat, and the battling block where the clothes

were "battled." All of this was grouped around a well, which was dug especially for supplying water for the washhouse.

When washday rolled around, my daddy would get things underway by drawing water and filling the wash pot, then he would build a roaring fire in the furnace. By the time the water was boiling my mother had the dirty clothes gathered up. She would first chip up a large quantity of Octagon soap into the pot, then add the clothes.

As the clothes boiled in the soapy water they were agitated by stirring them with a wood paddle, which was also used to lift them out of the pot and carry them to the battling block where they were pounded with another wood paddle to help get the dirt loose.

While all this was going on, someone else was busy filling the big wash tubs with clear water, (after the old water was dipped out), so the clothes could be rinsed and hung on the line.

It was truly an arduous and burdensome chore. Washday was one long hard day of backbreaking toil. No wonder we wore our overalls until they were stiff!

I'm sure thankful for the modern gadgets which have liberated today's wives and mothers from the old wash pot, the battling block, and rub board. And now, even from the clothes line!

Ash Hoppers

Some of you older readers will remember the old ash hopper which used to be a prominent fixture around homes back in the good ole days.

But most folks who are middle-aged or younger have never even seen or heard of an ash hopper, unless they've heard older folks reminiscing about it. The ash hopper was used to make lye for homemade lye soap, and here's how it worked:

Folks would save all the ashes from burning hickory wood in the fireplace, and they were put in the ash hopper during the wintertime. Then about March they would start putting a bucket of water in the top of the ash hopper each night. Soon the lye water would start running down a trough at the bottom of the hopper. The lye water would be caught in a bucket and put in an old black wash pot.

About the time the moon newed in April and May they would gather up all the old meat scraps they had saved during the winter, put them in the washpot with lye water and start cooking them. This would make enough lye soap to do until the following spring. The soap was cut into blocks when it was cooled and hardened, and that's what they used on washday. It would sure remove the dirt from overalls and other work clothes. And it would also remove the hide from around your fingernails, too!

There was another important thing that homemade lye was used for that all you country folks of generations past will recall, and that was to make hominy.

The grains of corn were soaked in the lye, which ate the husks and outer shell off the corn, leaving the soft center for delicious hominy, after it had been washed thoroughly to remove the lye, then cooked.

It was always a big job to wash the hominy because it had to go through so many rinsings with water drawn by hand from a dug well. But the reward came in eating the hominy — was it good!

I remember that my mother always made a big batch of hominy at a time and stored it in jars covered with water. And she always shared it with the neighbors, giving each neighbor a big mess of fresh hominy.

We can still buy hominy at the grocery store today, of course. But all of you who remember that good homemade hominy will agree that today's bought stuff can't touch it in taste with a ten-foot pole!

Shuck Mops

A fellow asked me the other day if I remembered what a shuck mop was like.

Do I! Why, I've used a many of one to clean floors with!

When I was a boy the shuck mop was a standard piece of housekeeping equipment in all respectable households, just as surely as a conventional mop is today.

One of the biggest compliments a housekeeper could receive was for someone to say "her floors are clean enough to eat off of." And that old shuck mop was the very way to clean them like that!

For you underprivileged people who don't know what we're talking about, here's how the shuck mop was made: Take a wide heavy board about a foot and half long, stick a hoe handle in it, bore about a dozen one-inch holes in the board and stuff corn shucks in the holes.

When we got ready to make a shuck mop we would go to the corncrib and select an armful of bright clean corn shucks. We would soak them in water until they were soft and pliable, then stuff them tightly in each hole. The pointed ends of the shucks protruded from the top and the heavy part of the shucks formed a thick mat on the underside, which was applied to the floor.

Washday was the best time for scrubbing the kitchen floor because several tubs or washpots of hot soapy water were available. You just dipped the mop in the water and started scrubbing until the bright grain of the wood in the floor could be seen. Usually some lye was added too, unless you were using homemade lye soap to start with.

Frequently, some clean white sand was thrown on the floor as an extra cleaning agent.

Now, all that was needed was plenty of elbow grease applied to the mop handle. Sometimes we put a couple of heavy flat irons on top of the mop for added weight.

There was no problem with the surplus water. It just ran out through the cracks in the floor!

Of course, it did take quite a bit of rinse water to complete the cleaning process, and that meant lots more elbow grease applied to the windlass drawing water from the well and toting it to the house.

If you remember only the bright clean floor, the old shuck mop was a fine piece of floor cleaning equipment. But if you get to thinking about all the elbow grease that was involved, it sort of puts a crimp in your fond memories about the good ole days!

Grist Mills

One of my favorite memories from the good ole days is taking corn to the grist mill to get it ground into meal.

This is a totally foreign experience for today's generations because the old timey grist mill as we knew it back then is now a thing of the past. Today we buy cornmeal at the grocery store and we miss out on some of the sights, sounds and tastes of fresh ground cornmeal back in the good ole days.

I'll never forget how the warm cornmeal smelled as it came out of the hopper after having been crushed between the heavy millstones. It smelled so good that I could never resist the temptation to pick up a handful and eat it right fresh out of the mill. And it tasted almost as good as it smelled!

Recently I visited an old water-powered grist mill that is still in operation, and it was something special to see all that enormous conglomeration of ponderous machinery going once again — just like in the good ole days.

A dam is located just above the mill there on a little creek, and a raceway carries the water down to the mill, ending in a wooden sluiceway which delivers the water directly above the huge mill wheel.

Just as I remembered it from the past, the miller is an old gentleman who has been running that mill for over 50 years, and he obviously knows every click and squeak about the whole operation. Typically, his clothes, his hat and his whiskers were white with cornmeal dust.

I watched him as he got ready to crank up the mill to grind a batch for a customer who had come in with some sacks of shelled corn. First he weighed the corn and deducted his grist (or toll). Then he darted up to the sluiceway and turned a wheel to open the sluice gate. This started a tremendous rush of water over and down across the old moss-covered wheel.

The rushing water, with a loud roar and much sloshing and splashing, quickly filled the compartments on the mill wheel and it began to turn — slowly at first but gradually over and over faster until it reached full speed.

Of course, full speed wasn't very fast. And that's the secret as to why water-ground meal is better. It is ground more slowly than is corn which is ground in motor-powered grist mills. Thus the meal does not get as hot in the grinding process.

Anyway, when the old mill wheel got up to full speed the miller dumped a measure of corn into the hopper, which in turn shook it down into the mill rocks. And slowly the newly ground meal began coming through into the collecting hopper, ready to be bagged and carried away or sold.

And yes, that fresh newly-ground meal tasted almost like it did when I was a boy! But the REAL taste treat comes when that new-ground meal turns up in a big pone of cornbread with a fresh glass of cold milk at the supper table!

Watering Troughs

How many of you remember the watering troughs which used to be a familiar fixture on the streets of country towns?

Back in the days before automobiles, when folks came to town in mule-drawn wagons and horse-drawn buggies, the public watering troughs were very important. The trip to town was a long one, and it took a lot of drinking water to quench the thirst of the horses and mules, especially in hot weather.

So the watering trough was a popular place, along with the hitching posts all along the streets. Every country courthouse had one or more watering troughs and a lot of hitching posts in front and behind, to accommodate the folks who came to the county seat to transact business.

People had to have their thirsts quenched also. And so there was frequently a hand pump next to the main watering trough in front of the courthouse or in the town square. There, one could pump a drink of fresh water, letting the excess run into the watering trough for his trusty steed.

And along country roads, it was a common thing for people to have hand pumps in wooded springs, where thirsty travelers could stop and get a drink of cool spring water as they passed by. On washdays, busy women could be found there by the spring washing clothes.

We had such a spring on our farm, and when our wells would go dry in the late summer or early fall we would haul water in barrels on a ground slide to the house to use for drinking purposes and for watering our livestock.

Even after the automobile made the public watering troughs and hitching posts obsolete, they continued to be favorite gathering places in country towns.

Now, though, they have disappeared from the scene, along with the old oaken buckets, gourd dippers and village blacksmiths. They've been replaced by drive-in fast food establishments, parking lots and service stations.

And without them, life in the country will never be the same!

Washholes

One of the most popular places in every town and community (and in many backyards) during the summertime is the swimming pool. Back in the good ole days, it was the community washhole.

That was before the days when creeks and streams were contaminated and filled with all kinds of litter. And every country creek had a place in it where the water was ponded several feet deep — just right for a washhole.

It always had overhanging trees along the banks, and those trees generally had some big strong old wild muscadine vines growing high into the top branches —just the thing for swinging out on and dropping into the water. The diving board was a big stump along the creek bank.

And since there were no dressing rooms, we just showed up with the duds we were going swimming in, then went home with our wet clothes on. Our swimming suit was usually an old pair of overalls with the legs cut off above the knees.

And if the swimming hole wasn't too close to a road, we boys would often just shuck our clothes and go skinny dipping, provided there were no girls around. However, this sometimes caused a problem if girls or womenfolks showed up unexpectedly. And many's the time an embarrassed country boy had to just stay hunkered in the water for hours, until everybody left or nightfall came.

One of the favorite stunts in those days was to catch somebody skinny dipping, snatch his clothes from the bank and run off with them. The victim would have to wait until after dark to sneak home, unless someone came with clothes to rescue him.

But washholes were a whole lot of fun. And they were always popular summertime gathering places in every community on Saturday and Sunday afternoons.

Just about every rural community had a famous washhole, where big gatherings would take place on such special occasions as the Fourth of July — right along with the picnics, barbecues and cow pasture baseball games.

What excitement it was to swing high out over the water from a muscadine vine or plowline tied up on a tree limb, making a bodacious splash into the water. But there could be a painful surprise waiting when you hit the muddy bottom, if there was a tree root lurking down there!

Today's cement ponds with their clear filtered water are a big improvement over those old washholes of the good ole days. But not one bit more fun!

Saturday Night Baths

Today's kids who fuss about having to take a bath every night might find cause to envy those of a few generations ago, if they knew that the first bathtub built in the United States was made in Cincinnati in 1842.

It was constructed of mahogany, lined with sheet lead, and it was exhibited at a Christmas party.

The next day the local newspaper denounced it as a "luxurious and undemocratic vanity." Doctors warned that the bathtub would be "a menace to health."

The next year, in 1843, Philadelphia undertook by public ordinance to prohibit bathing between November 1 and March 15. And two years later, Boston made bathing unlawful except when prescribed by a physician.

Well, by the time I came along folks were real hung up on the idea of taking baths on a regular basis. We kids had to take a bath every Saturday night, whether we needed one or not!

Our bathtub was a much simpler one, however. It was the same old galvanized washtub that my mother rinsed clothes in every Monday.

After supper was finished on Saturday night, the dishes were washed and everybody had adjourned to the porch or the "big house" (our living and sleeping quarters) to rock and talk til bedtime. It was time for us kids to take our bath.

The big tub was stationed in the middle of the kitchen floor in front of the fireplace if it was winter or on the back porch if it was summer (after dark, of course).

Water was brought from the well to partially fill the tub, with warm water added from the reservoir of the Home Comfort range. A big amber-colored bar of Octagon soap and a flour sack wash rag were readied, and it was time for the bath-taking to begin.

Hunkering and squatting in that tub involved considerable dexterity. But we didn't know any better, so to us it was a part of the process. And when each bather was through, he stepped out on the floor and dried off with a flour sack or fertilizer sack towel.

The oldest child always got to take a bath first, and so on down the line.

Well, I was the youngest. And when you have four older siblings, the bath water gets to looking a little funny by the time it's your turn! But when you have to draw water out of a well in the yard and bring it in a bucketful at a time, you sure don't change the water after every bath!

Looking back on it now, I can see that we probably DID need that bath every Saturday night, after we had worked in the dusty fields all week. Especially if we had not had a chance to skinny-dip in the washhole down at the creek.

But if I had been a qualified voter at the time, I probably would have voted for one of those anti-bathing ordinances!

Ole Timey Remedies

When I was growing up in the good ole days, folks generally didn't head for the doctor or the drug store for treatment or medicines when "everyday" illness struck. They just reached up on the mantel over the fireplace, where they kept their largely-homemade stuff for treating whatever it was that ailed them.

Back in the days before anybody ever heard of viruses, antibiotics or vitamin pills, every family had its own "tried and true" remedies for every ailment, and many of them were strictly homemade!

The standard remedy for a hacking cough at our house was a teaspoon of sugar with a few drops of kerosene in it. When I started coughing in the middle of the night, my mother would soon come with the kerosene-soaked sugar fixed up and ready for instant use during the "colds and coughing season."

Many's the time I have jumped out of the barn and stuck a rusty nail in my foot. Instead of rushing me to the doctor for a tetanus shot, my mother just soaked my foot in a pan of hot water with salts in it, then saturated the wound with terpentine.

Years ago a woman told me that one of the remedies in their community for a nail-stuck foot was to burn woolen rags in an old bucket and hold the afflicted foot over the smoke for awhile.

Springtime brought on the need (my parents thought) for a tonic. And sassafras tea was the universal choice. Every roadside had sassafras plants growing on the ditch banks, so it was easy to dig up the roots and boil them to make sassafras tea. I've drunk many gallons of it in my time.

Another sure thing when spring rolled around was sulfur and molasses, which was supposed to be good for a number of ills. One reason it cured kids was that it tasted so bad that we didn't dare get puny for fear of having to take more of the stuff!

Taking medicine is never fun. But I suppose most of today's store-bought medicines are less obnoxious than our homemade ones were. That's easy for me to say, though, since I'm not a kid anymore!

The Family Doctor

Few things have changed more in these modern times from the way they used to be in the good ole days than the appearances, methods and modes of practice by the family doctor.

When I was growing up way out in the country, we seldom went to the doctor. In fact, we seldom went anywhere. Going to town was a rare experience. We grew most of our food at home, and the few things we had to buy were purchased either from peddlers or rolling stores or in big quantities once or twice year. Thus, when we got sick, we called the doctor and he came to our house.

You older folks will remember that in most cases, when automobiles were a rarity, it was usually the local doctor in a town who owned the first automobile. Doctors always had the finest horses and buggies around. They needed the best in transportation, because they had to get to their patients.

I can remember numerous times when the doctor would come to our house when someone in the family was sick, and he would sit by the bedside for hours, sometimes even all night, until the "crisis" had passed.

Oftentimes he probably knew little more to do than check the fever and perhaps give an aspirin occasionally. But his presence there by the bedside was a great assurance both to the patient and to the rest of the family.

Every doctor carried with him a big black bag, which was not only filled with the tools of his trade but also was stocked with medicines. And instead of whipping out a pad and scribbling a prescription to be carried to the drug store and filled, he just issued the medicine right there on the spot.

Our family doctor used to sometimes laugh and tell us how often he had given people "sugar pills" when he went to see them or they came to see him, and he could find nothing whatsoever organically wrong with them. And the "nothing" pills seemed to cure them just fine in most such cases.

Doctors' offices in those days looked a little like a drugstore might look today, in an old fashioned motif. I can remember going to the office of our family doctor and seeing those massive jars of medicines on high shelves on the sides of his office. He mixed most of his medicines right there in his office.

In these days, of course, the medicines have changed even more than the methods. And none of us want to go back to the old timey things.

It would be ridiculous to suggest that today's busy doctors could or should forsake the confines of their well-equipped offices or the medically sophisticated atmosphere of a modern hospital to just sit in a bedroom all night holding the hand of a critically ill patient.

But the need for loving concern has not changed. And to any degree that we have lost this doctor-patient relationship, we've lost something that no modern medicines or methods can replace.

"An Apple A Day"

If we could turn the clock and calendar back about 75 years or more, we would discover that life was much simpler than it is in this modern space age.

Folks didn't have nearly as much formal education, as a rule. Our society was still populated largely by folks who had grown up close to the land, even if they themselves had left the country.

There were no things as jet airplanes, space ships, computers, satellites and television. Even radio itself was still unknown.

Life moved at a slower pace, and folks still had time to visit their neighbors and socialize together in neighborhoods. They also had time to observe more of the things around them, learning from nature and natural cycles many of the things they needed to know for daily living.

I came along a bit later than this, but in the simple country atmosphere in which I grew up, there was still much of this sort of thing left in folks' lives, including many practices and sayings which had evolved from those good ole days.

Neither of my parents had much formal education. But as I grew older I began to realize that their native wisdom put lots of my "book learning" in the shade! For example, my daddy was a great believer in the old saying that "an apple a day keeps the doctor away," and he always made it a practice to eat an apple every afternoon.

Now, nutritionists are touting apples as one of our greatest health foods. And the other day I picked up a catalog from a health food center which extolled apple pectin tablets made from fresh apples as "a natural digestive aid." The article went on to explain that apple pectin "nutures and promotes the growth of intestinal flora beneficial to digestion, promotes inner cleanliness and may be a natural anti-toxin against inner pollution."

A registered dietitian in a major medical clinic told me recently that she strongly recommends eating apples regularly. She says they are an excellent source of needed dietary fiber, and that apple pectin can help lower cholesterol levels.

My daddy always had us put the hardwood ashes from our fireplace around our apple trees. I thought it was just a curious notion of his. But when I studied horticulture in college I learned that apple trees thrive on the ingredients they get from such ashes.

In this age of great enlightenment, there is still much we can learn from the simple ways and simple days of long ago. Another reason for remembering those good ole days.

Sassafrass Tea

When I was growing up, one thing that I could always count on when spring rolled around was that my mother would start brewing up a batch of sassafras tea and insist that we kids drink this for a while to make sure we were hale and hearty for the busy summer ahead.

It seemed like sassafras grew wild on just about every road bank and bare hillside. And it was always a regular thing for folks in the spring of the year to go out and dig up sassafras roots and boil up a big batch of sassafras tea. It was supposed to give everybody lots of pep and energy and help them overcome the blahs of a long hard winter.

Well, I hear tell that some folks have revived this practice. And they've found that sassafras tea is not so bad after all. (Like I used to think it was when my mother made me drink so much of it).

Now, there may be still another reason for drinking sassafras tea, what with coffee prices as high as a cat's back. And tea prices are not much better these days, either. In fact, one home economist is suggesting that folks try sassafras tea as a possible drink instead of regular tea or coffee.

Several years ago I heard about some enterprising fellows who got hold of a piece of land with lots of sassafras bushes growing on it. They took a bulldozer and dug up those sassafras roots, ground them up and packaged them and started selling them in supermarkets for folks who wanted to make sassafras tea.

But I wonder if they really got rich at it. Lots of folks might have been like me. I couldn't resist buying a package and brewing some sassafras tea to see if it still tasted like it did when I was a boy. Yep, it tasted about the same. Somewhere in between a dose of medicine and a cup of plain hot water.

However, I don't question the fact that sassafras tea would be a lot cheaper to drink than coffee or regular tea, for those who care to find some wild sassafras bushes growing and dig up their own.

And I don't question the fact that a good hot cup of sassafras tea is good for whatever ails you. At least, I wouldn't have dared question this when I was growing up, when my daddy prescribed it for me every spring. If I had, I would sure as the world have had something ailing me right quick! Like a sore bottom!

Beauty Aids

Lots of things are different in these modern times from the way they used to be back in the good ole days.

Back then, folks couldn't buy everything like they can nowadays. And even after lots of things got to being for sale in stores, we poor folks didn't have the money to buy them. So we had to keep on doing without, or making up our own homemade things.

Take cosmetics, for example. Back then the women folks were just as concerned about being pretty as they are today, though they didn't have all the fancy bought things to put on their bodies to help make them that way.

But they didn't let that fact slow them down any. They just figured out their own homemade concoctions, which worked pretty well.

For eye bags and dark circles under the eyes, they would put grated raw potatoes over their eyes and relax for about 15 minutes. This was applied directly as a poultice or put in cloth sacks.

Freckles were removed (hopefully) by applying a paste made of eggs, cream and Epsom salts. It was left on the face until it dried, then washed off.

A wrinkle cream was made by mixing two table-spoons of fresh cream with one teaspoon of honey, stirred and applied to the face. It was allowed to dry, and then the face was rinsed with water. I don't know how many wrinkles it actually removed, but it must have been very interesting in appearance and very enticing to flies!

A hair rinse was often made by mixing three table-spoons of vinegar to a cup of warm water, to give softness and gloss to the hair.

And a favorite sunburn remedy was made with the white of an egg beaten and whipped together with one teaspoon of castor oil, then applied to the skin.

"Necessity is the mother of invention," as the old saying goes. To women of all ages, looking pretty has been considered a necessity. (And I sure don't hear any men objecting to that idea).

So, women have always come up with the necessary beauty concoctions, whether they were able to buy them or whether they had to just make them up for themselves.

Many beauty secrets were handed down from mothers and grandmothers, as they still are. And probably one of the greatest of these was and is: "Beauty is as beauty does!"

Homemade Ice Cream

One of the most satisfying pleasures this old world has to offer is that of eating homemade ice cream fresh out of the freezer on a hot summer day!

When I was growing up, we could always tell who was planning to make ice cream on Saturday night by watching the cars go by on Saturday afternoon, on the way home from town.

Folks who were planning that Saturday evening ritual would stop by the ice plant in town the last thing before heading toward home. They would buy a block of ice and tie it to the rear bumper with binder twine, then rush home before the ice melted.

While the woman of the house went to the kitchen to mix up the ice cream solution, the menfolks would head to the back porch with that prized block of frozen water to crush it and get it ready for the freezer.

The ice was placed in a burlap bag (commonly called a "croker sack") and beat it with the flat side of a double-bit ax until it was crushed finely enough to go into the freezer bucket.

Then came the long process of cranking the freezer until it got so hard to turn that we knew the ice cream was made. We never could be patient enough to pack it and let it set and mellow and continue hardening for awhile, because we were anxious to get on with the eating.

And I never did figure out how all our neighbors happened to drop by for a visit just about the time the ice cream was made!

Ice was such a precious commodity in the summertime! We had no electricity out in the country when I was growing up, and thus no refrigerator. Home

freezers, of course, had not been invented. So we let our milk down into the well to keep it cool. And we sometimes brought cool water from a nearby spring.

We did figure out some ways to keep ice for a few days, by packing it in sawdust or cottonseed, or wrapping it in blankets. That way, we could make a 100 pound block of ice last for several days.

Later, we finally managed to obtain an old wooden ice box to keep foods cool in. The ice went into an insulated compartment on top, with a drain pipe running through to the bottom and through a hole in the porch floor, allowing it to drip under the house. Who could ever have imagined making our own ice right in the refrigerator — much less the frozen foods that we take for granted today!

But nobody has ever figured out a way to beat that good old homemade ice cream, made in a hand-cranked freezer on the back porch on Saturday night or the 4th of July!

All Day Singings
(And Dinner On The Ground)

There are lots of things that we can look forward to with the arrival of springtime each year. Things like spring cleaning, hay fever and outdoor barbecues. And, all day singings with dinner on the ground.

Now, I could devote this entire space and much more to the singing part of it. But I'm going to concentrate on my favorite part — the dinner on the ground. Dinners on the ground, of course, not only go with all day singings in the summertime, but they also go with such get-togethers as decoration days and family reunions.

The idea is that each family will bring enough food for themselves, plus some extra. All the food will be spread on big tables and benches out under the shade trees. And everybody will load up their plates and eat and eat until they can't eat any more. While they're eating, they will talk and talk until everything there is to talk about will have been said.

While the womenfolks clean up the leftover food and pack it away to take home, the kids will play games and the menfolks will talk some more.

It seldom ever fails to be the case that more food is packed up and taken home than was eaten. What happens is that each woman wants to make sure that there is plenty of food to go around. So, instead of cooking enough for her family plus a little extra, she brings enough for her family plus about 10 other families.

I've been to lots of dinners on the ground where there would be so many different kinds of meat that I couldn't have taken even just a bite from each batch. Likewise for the salads, vegetables and desserts. And

95

that didn't even take into consideration what the ants and flies got!

Not only is the quantity of food a concern with such cooks. But when a woman is baking something to take to a dinner on the ground, her cooking reputation is sort of on the line. So, you may rest assured that her favorite and most famous concoctions will show up on that table.

Yes, dinners on the ground are a favorite tradition. And who am I to want to interfere with tradition!

Front Porches

I've noticed that folks are starting to build more new houses with big front porches on them again. It makes me think that we have finally figured out what all we've been missing since porches started disappearing from our houses a few decades ago.

Back in the good ole days, every home had a huge front porch that stretched all the way across the front of the house. And it was deep enough to make room for a swing, one or two tables, several rocking chairs and an assortment of other things — not counting a bed for the family dog to sleep on.

In fact, if you go all the way back to the big houses built prior to World War I you'll find many of them with porches all the way around the house. And some of the houses, especially in the rural areas, had a "dog trot" or open porch or hallway splitting the middle of the house as well — separating the eating and lounging area from the sleeping area.

This latter design evolved from the practice in olden times of building the kitchen entirely separate from the rest of the house. Back then, families still cooked in open fireplaces and kitchen fires were quite common. Hopefully, if the kitchen burned down the rest of the family quarters could be saved.

As the years went by, changing architectural designs shifted porches around a lot, first to the sides of the house and then to the rear. Eventually, even back porches began to disappear in favor of patios. Then there were screened-in back porches, covered patios, etc.

But through all the shifts and changes, nothing has ever matched the wonderful joys provided by the outdoor living area on the big front porch.

Lots of courting was done in the front porch swing during the pleasant afternoons and evenings of spring and summer Saturdays and Sundays.

If you lived in town, there was no place to watch a parade like your front porch. And whether you lived in town or in the country, you could always see the "parade" of comings and goings best from your front porch. Sitting in a big rocking chair on the front porch and watching the world go by was practically guaranteed to make you relax and forget your troubles.

And if you were traveling down the street or a country road, you could see all your friends and neighbors and holler and wave to them as you passed — especially if you were walking, riding in a wagon or buggy or tooling along in your Model T.

Well, the front porch is making a comeback. And I think it will help to cure many of the ills of our modern society. Especially if folks will get back out onto those porches, where they belong!

Back Porches

Before the days of running water and indoor bathrooms, the back porch was the scene of much daily activity.

For example, it was the place where everybody washed their hands and got a drink of water. And when folks came in with dirty shoes, they sat down on the back steps and took them off, leaving them on the back porch when they went into the house.

Every back porch had a table or high bench with a wash pan or wash basin on it. And next to it sat a water bucket which was taken out to the well to be refilled as needed.

By (or in) the water bucket was a dipper, made of tin, or fashioned out of a gourd. Everybody drank out of the same dipper when they wanted a drink of water. And the water was dipped out and into the wash pan as needed. Then the dirty water was tossed out into the yard. A clean flour sack towel always hung there ready for hands and face to be dried.

Some folks got affluent and fancy enough to buy a hand pump. And so they would dig a well right by the back porch and mount the pump there. Then, anytime they wanted some water all they had to do was put the dipper, pan or bucket under the spout, give the pump handle a few vigorous pumps, and they had water fresh out of the well!

We never had such a marvelous gadget at our house. But I had a friend whose family had a hand pump, and I always loved to go to his house and pump water right there on the back porch. What a thrill!

Some families had all of this on their front porch instead of their back porch. Especially if they had a pump. That way, everybody who passed could plainly see that they weren't quite as poor as the rest of us!

Later on came another gadget that totally revolutionized washdays. The wringer washer. A few families out in the country, before we got electricity out there, bought gasoline-powered models.

But as rural electrification brought the power lines to the farm, wringer washers that were electrically powered began to appear on front porches and back porches everywhere. Thankfully, washday drudgery was on its way out!

You talk about affluence and luxury! Driving down the road and seeing your neighbor with a new washing machine on the porch really made an impression! But wringer washers quickly became a necessity rather than a luxury. And most older women today can quickly tell you the very day they got their first one.

Soon came automatic water pumps, running water and indoor bathrooms. Life in the country was never the same again. Thank goodness!

Home Comforts

Driving around through a modern subdivision the other day and looking at the beautiful homes which have been built in recent years, I got to thinking about how different they are from the house that I grew up in and how housing designs have changed since back there in the good ole days!

I was born and raised in the same house that my daddy was born and raised in. In fact, it started out as a log house that was built by my grandfather when he returned from the Civil War and settled our old homeplace.

In those days the kitchen was in a separate building, separated from the rest of the house by a space of several yards. The primary reason for this, I believe, was as a safety factor against fire. You see, most of the cooking was originally done on fireplaces, and later in big wrought iron wood-burning stoves, and the danger of setting the house on fire was greater in the kitchen than in the rest of the house.

Later, when houses got more modern, the entire house was built together, but there was a wide hallway all the way through the center of the house, commonly called a "dog trot."

Our old homeplace, however, had the kitchen separate, connected by a covered walkway which we called "the crossway." This crossway was entirely open on the sides, with bannisters along the sides, and on a cold winter morning the wind would whip across it something fierce!

I can remember how I used to crawl out of bed before daylight on a cold morning, grab my clothes and make a mad dash to the kitchen to get dressed in front of the roaring fire in the big kitchen fireplace.

Barefooted, and dressed only in my "union suit" or "long handles," I could set some kind of track record for the 25-yard dash getting from a cold bedroom to that hot fire!

My daddy would get up at 4 o'clock every morning and head for the kitchen to build a fire in the fireplace and in that big Home Comfort stove, so that by the time Mother got to the kitchen she was ready to make the biscuits and fry the ham, while Daddy went to the barn and shucked the corn and fed the cows and mules.

Those of us who grew up in those kinds of houses certainly know how to appreciate today's modern housing comforts. Especially when we get out of bed on a cold winter morning in a house that is comfortably heated, get dressed and enjoy a family breakfast before we have to brave the cold winter winds.

There are some things about that old homeplace that I long for and miss. But one of them is not crawling out of bed on a cold winter morning!

Air Conditioning

Of all the contrivances for modern living, few have changed our living patterns more than the air conditioner.

Now, during extremely hot weather, most of us stay comfortable in our air conditioned houses, workplaces and cars most of the day. And we sleep comfortably at night, oblivious of the outdoors heat.

Back in the good ole days, before air conditioning, folks sat on their porches and out under the shade trees on hot summer days. When they went to church or to a funeral or other public gathering they fanned themselves with cardboard fans. These fans were usually supplied by the local funeral home, which had its name prominently displayed on the back of the fan. The front always had a color picture of a pretty scene or a drawing of the face of Jesus.

Out in the country, we didn't have any fancy pews in our churches, like the city folks had. Instead, we had benches made out of pine. And I'll never forget how those white flour sack shirts, wet with perspiration, would stick to those pine slats on the benches, leaving yellow steaks across the back of the shirt.

In the home, doors and windows were kept open all during the summer, to let the cooling breezes in. This meant lots of flies in the house, through holes in the screens and opening of the doors.

Of course, many people today work in places that are not air conditioned. And many homes are not air conditioned. But at least, most homes and commercial buildings have insulation to help keep out the heat. And there aren't nearly as many of those tin roofs like we used to have which literally soaked up the sun's heat and conveyed it straight down onto us below.

I suppose that back in the days before air condition-ing, we just endured it and didn't think much about how miserable or uncomfortable we were. Besides, there wasn't much we could do about it anyway.

Ah, yes! Those were the good ole days! They're interesting to remember. But every time I think about them on a hot summer day, I cuddle up to the nearest air conditioner or cool air vent and give thanks for that modern invention which keeps us cool on the hottest of days!

Rolling Stores

When I was a boy growing up out in the country back in the good ole days, one of the most exciting times of the week was the day when the rolling store "ran."

Rolling stores, those unique stores on wheels, were a real institution in all rural communities back in those days.

Just about every community was served by one or more rolling stores, and they came around on a regular schedule each week. This was a real service to rural families because it was difficult for folks to get to town to buy necessities, and a few minor luxuries now and then.

For those of you who never saw a rolling store, it was just what the name implies. It was a small store mounted on the back of a truck. The walls were lined with shelves stocked with daily use items ranging all the way from lard to sewing thread.

Fastened to the top or back of the truck were several chicken coops, always filled with squawking chickens which folks along the route traded for items they wanted or needed.

It was a regular thing for us kids to rob the hens' nests to gather up a few extra eggs to have to trade for candy or chewing gum when the rolling store came around each week. And what an exciting adventure it was to climb up and peek inside the rolling store, laden with all sorts of goodies!

Living eight miles out in the country, a long trip by wagon on dirt roads, going to town took all day. So we didn't get to go much.

Most of our basic food items were raised at home, such as our meat, milk and eggs. We even grew our own

wheat and had our own flour milled, at times. And of course, we grew our own corn and had it ground into meal for our cornbread. But things like sugar, spice, salt, and coffee had to be bought, and these usually came from the rolling store.

Lots of times we got a few special treats, such as a slab of hoop cheese and some soda crackers, maybe even a can of sardines. And for the adults who indulged in such things there was the weekly supply of smoking tobacco, chewing tobacco and snuff.

Rolling stores did not become obsolete until the early 1960s, so many young adults still remember them.

For those of us who are middle age or older, the rolling store is a favorite memory from our childhood days, and it saddens me a bit to think of its demise.

Fixing The Roads

We're all the time hearing and reading about highway taxes and road building funds, and it seems there's never enough to go around.

How many of you remember the way roads used to be kept up back in the good ole days? Every property owner was required to give at least one day's work every year on the roads. He either had to do the work himself or hire someone to do it for him.

I can remember when my daddy and other neighbor men would work on the roads, using tools and methods that were mighty crude by today's standards. Dirt was moved with hand-held mule-drawn pans in the days before heavy road machines. That was a little before my time, but I can still remember this equipment being used. Dirt was also hauled sometimes on a ground slide. And, of course, shovels, picks, and hoes were common tools for road building and maintenance.

There were no problems relating to pavement because we didn't have any paved roads in those days out in the country where I lived. And, of course, road needs and demands were much simpler in the days of wagons, buggies and Model T Fords than they are today.

Nevertheless, the roads still had to be built and maintained. And it was done largely with human labor by farmers who applied to this task the same kind of common sense and hard labor that they were accustomed to using on their farms.

The work was done mainly at times and seasons when labor demands were slack in the fields. And if a heavy rain washed out the road by a fellow's place, he just got out and fixed it himself.

I'm sure not advocating going back to that sort of way of building and maintaining roads. Besides, it would be impossible to do it that way in these modern times.

But I wish we could recapture some of the innovative, do-it-yourself spirit which characterized more people in those days than it does today.

And somehow, it appears, we're going to have to come up — in these modern times — with some innovative ideas for maintaining our roads and streets. As I keep busy dodging potholes, enduring bumps and frequenting the front-end-alignment shops, I'm about to decide that there's not enough money in the entire world to pay for fixing our roads again!

Helping Your Neighbors

You can find yourself lost in just about any strange neighborhood these days, and lots of times it gets frustrating when you're looking for a particular family or individual and people you stop to ask don't know them — even though they may live just a few hundred yards away.

It is one of the realities of modern times that neighbors just aren't as "close" as they used to be back in the good ole days.

These times that we live in are so fast-paced and we all have so many distractions that keep us from interacting with people around us like previous generations did. It is unfortunate, I think, that we just don't get together and visit and help each other out like folks used to do.

I have been thinking anew on this as I have been reflecting back on the days of barn raisings, wood cuttings, quilting bees and Saturday night get-togethers which were so much a part of my growing-up days.

In those days we didn't have such entertainment as television. We didn't have cars to go here and yonder in. We didn't have recreational facilities and programs provided by local government agencies and groups. And we weren't all that busy either.

So, we concocted our own entertainment. We got together and worked and played and helped each other more than folks do today.

If a man got sick, his neighbors saw to it that his crops got made, that his family had plenty of firewood and stovewood cut for the winter, and that other pressing family needs were taken care of.

111

Nobody ever thought about getting paid for such things; it was just the neighborly thing to do. And besides, they knew they could count on the same thing if they ever got down and out.

When the crops had been gathered in the fall, we would get together for wood cutting on the different farms in the community, to help each other lay in a supply of firewood for the winter.

Now, folks look more to the government to help them when they're in need. I'm not so sure that we ought to call this progress, however!

Log Rollings

Changing times have resulted in the disappearance of many customs which used to characterize life in rural areas back in the good ole days.

One of these customs which younger generations know nothing about is log rollings, which once were staged in every rural community during the fall and winter months.

The purpose of a log rolling was to help a farmer clear out some of his timber and at the same time cut his winter's supply of firewood and stovewood.

When someone got ready to host a log rolling, they would announce it in the community several weeks ahead of time. On the week of the event, the host would go into the woods and fell several big trees, harvest some of his best apples, parch up a big batch of peanuts and prepare for a huge bonfire.

Right after suppertime on the night of the log rolling, folks from all over the community would gather for the big event. The men and older boys would head straight for the woods with their crosscut saws and axes, while the women began preparing refreshments. The children would begin their games around the bonfire in the front yard.

After a couple of hours of hard work, the trees would be sawed up and the wood split, so the workers headed back to the house.

There was plenty of good eating, story telling, game playing, and maybe some music making and singing for another hour or so until time for everyone to head for their homes.

While a log rolling was a way for neighbors to help each other with work which one family alone could not get done, it was also a major social get-together.

Similar events like barn raisings and corn shuckings were more in the former category, though people in those days managed to make them fun along with the work.

Every community had some people who were pretty good at "making music." So there was never any shortage of talent for picking and singing!

It was a time also when people had very little money to spend. We grew our own food, made things that we needed, and did without most everything else. Certainly there was not much money for hiring labor on the farm.

Out of this kind of life, however, came a spirit of neighborliness which has been pretty much lost in our modern days.

And with this loss has come the disappearance of a way of life which, sadly, will never return!

Quiltin' Parties

Recently I enjoyed visiting with a young couple in their new log home. It was a lot different from the old log houses such as the one I was born and raised in. But while it was very modern in every respect, I was interested to see that these young people have carefully preserved some of the things that they doubtless learned from their parents and grandparents about the good ole days.

For instance, hanging on the wall above their bed was a beautiful old quilt, which was given to this young wife by her grandmother. As I admired this quilt and thought about all the loving work that had gone into it, I was remembering how important quilts have been in family life for so many generations.

It is interesting to note that lots of younger women are now re-discovering the joys of quilting.

Quilting parties used to be common events in most communties. In fact, they provided one of the major means of socializing for lots of women, who would gather in someone's home about once a week for a quilting party.

While the children played outside, the women would hunker around a big quilting frame in the middle of a bedroom or living room and quilt and gossip and enjoy each other's company. They would quit for a spread of lunch from everybody's basket, then go back to quilting until time to head for home in the afternoon.

In the days before comfortably heated houses and electric blankets, quilts were important for bed coverings. And every woman took pride in having a big supply of colorful and warm quilts on hand for her family at all times. No daughter was allowed to get married without her mother having made several fine quilts for her to take as a part of her dowry.

This is not as important as it used to be. But most families still have some of these quilts which have been passed along for several generations and are still used. A good quilt will last for several generations, if it is taken care of.

Quilting has become a favorite activity in many neighborhoods in recent years. And learning to quilt is now a fashionable and favorite pastime for many groups of young women.

Many of them tell me that making quilts is one of their favorite projects. There is much pleasure and a chance for fulfilling an urge for creativeness in designs, color combinations and quilting patterns. And what a way to use scraps from other sewing jobs!

It takes a lot of time, patience and attentiveness to fine detail to make a good quilt. These are things we've tended to cast aside in today's hustle-bustle world.

For many women, going back to the old quilting frame is one way to recapture some of the joys and satisfactions of the good ole days!

"Drummers"

How many of you remember the traveling salesmen or peddlers who used to visit farms and homes in the rural areas back during the good ole days?

Before the days of automobiles, when rural areas were sparsely settled, these "drummers," as they were commonly called, would come around on foot or on horseback or in a buggy, selling everything from buggy whips to beauty aids.

Folks didn't travel much in those days, and even going to town was just an occasional thing. News of the world was a scarce commodity for most families. So these much-traveled characters were a fascinating source of information.

They would make their way across the countryside, stopping to spend the night wherever they found a welcome when nightfall was approaching. They always had a vast store of tales to tell and news to relate. So they peddled their wares and dispensed their conversation all at the same time.

Some of them were preachers as well, and they spread the Gospel as they traveled across the countryside. But unfortunately, more of them were con men and shysters who were far more interested in emptying folks' pockets than in saving their soul.

Later, as cars came along, the peddlers began to travel in horseless carriages. This gave them considerably more mobility, and also made it possible for them to take in more things for trade. Money was scarce in those days, but most rural families had plenty of chickens and eggs and vegetables and meat. So folks would swap these things for the bought items they needed from the peddler.

While the automobile gave the peddler more mobility and enlarged his basis of operations, it also proved eventually to be his downfall, because people were enabled to travel more and to shop for themselves at the sources of supply.

But it was more than just a merchandising thing too. As radios, daily newspapers and other means of mass communication became commonplace in the home, there was no longer much demand for the stories and newsy tales of the peddlers.

So, like the horse and buggy, the "drummers" faded into oblivion and turned to other things. Some of them became traveling "medicine men" who peddled their wares and entertained crowds on street corners and courthouse yards in the towns. Others became traveling salesmen for manufacturers and wholesalers, calling primarily on merchants and industries.

Some of those who were preachers bought tents and began a new kind of revival ministry — or simply preached in brush arbors.

But in every case, the colorful activities of these drummers and preachers spanned several generations and left indelible memories in countless places back in the good ole days.

Lightning Rods

How long has it been since you've seen a lightning rod?

Going back a few decades, just about every house had one or more of these gadgets affixed to the roof. They were supposed to help protect the structure from being struck by lightning.

A lightning rod is simply a pointed metal rod extending all the way up from the ground and towering above the roof, or one that is attached to the top of the roof with a ground wire leading to the ground. If hit by a bolt of lightning it directs the lightning harmlessly into the ground, thus sparing the building.

Nowdays one can drive all over the countryside and never spot a lightning rod on a house. Every once in awhile, though, I see one still sticking up on top of an old barn somewhere.

This doesn't mean that folks don't have lightning rods, however. In fact, many modern structures are protected from lightning by a new version of the lightning rod, called a low voltage lightning arrestor.

In fact, I have one on my own house. But instead of a rod sticking up on top of the house, it is a round object about three or four times as big as a large biscuit, and it is integrated into the main electric line coming into my house. If lightning runs in on the service wires, this gadget is supposed to direct the damaging charge into the ground and keep it from burning up all my household appliances. Unfortunately, it doesn't always work!

These modern gadgets have just about put the notorious lightning rod salesmen of a generation ago out of business. But I can remember how these shysters used to travel around the countryside, looking for houses without lightning rods. When they spotted such a house, they would stop and unleash a hard-pressure sales pitch about the grave dangers of lightning striking and burning down an unprotected house.

After collecting a tidy sum of money, they would simply stick a cheap rod on top of the house, not even bothering to attach a ground wire. The whole thing, of course, was totally useless!

We still have our modern-day shyster salesmen of various sorts. But, as far as I know, this is not one of their current games!

Raising Chickens

Every time I visit one of today's giant poultry houses and see all the automatic and mechanized equipment and efficient management procedures I think of how different it is from the way we used to raise chickens back in the good ole days.

Back then every family had their own flock of chickens. And this wasn't just country folks either. City families often had their own chickens too, especially if they lived in a small town.

We didn't really have poultry houses in today's fashion. At least, we didn't keep the chickens cooped up during the day. The houses were really just roosting places and nesting places. During the day the chickens had free run of the yard.

This created a lot of interesting situations. For example, one had to be very careful where he stepped when he walked around the yard, and sometimes even across the front porch!

Gathering the eggs was quite an adventure, because — no matter what kind of nests were provided — many of the hens had their own notions about where they wanted to lay their eggs. And so they would often have their own nests under the house or barn or at some other out-of-the-way places.

This was especially true in the spring, when the old mother instinct became so strong that the hens would hide their nests so they could accumulate a nestful of eggs to set on and hatch a bunch of biddies.

Another adventurous thing was preparing a fresh fryer for a family meal. It wasn't a matter of going to the grocery store to buy a dressed fryer; it was a matter of stepping out into the yard and chasing down the

victim, wringing his neck, and picking and dressing him while the water was getting hot!

Now, poultry raising is so scientific, so automated, so efficient that our do-it-yourself system seems hard to imagine.

Back in those good ole days, it took farmers about 18 to 20 weeks to produce a fryer which would dress out at about two pounds. Now, with our modern chickens and production methods a commercial poultryman produces a finished bird more than twice that size in one third of the time.

And while we thought back then that those fryers were tasty and delicious, if we compared one of those with the modern broiler chicken that we eat today, we would realize that today's birds are much more tender and tasty than those from the good ole days.

Few industries in our nation's food production chain have come so far so fast as has the poultry business.

But just think of all the fun we're missing because we've taken our chickens out of the yard and off the front porch and put them in climate controlled automated "poultry factories!"

Settin' Hens

The other day I went on a tour of a modern hatchery, and the manager showed me through the hatching room with the huge incubators, explaining how these marvelous machines take thousands of eggs and turn them into baby chicks in 21 days.

He explained all of the elaborate temperature and humidity controls and showed me how the eggs are carefully rotated within the machine to make sure the yolks do not adhere to the inside of the egg shells during the incubating process.

"We can do a pretty good job with this hatching business," he said, "but with all of our expensive sophisticated equipment we still haven't figured out how to do it as efficiently as an old mother hen can do it in her own nest."

Well, I got to thinking about those old settin' hens that I had known through the years and some of the interesting experiences I used to have with them.

Back in the days when everybody let their chickens run loose, we played a grim game with the hens when spring approached. They would always hide their nests from us, then try to lay them full of eggs and set on them, to hatch out a family of biddies.

One of my jobs when I got home from school in the afternoon (besides bringing in stovewood) was gathering the eggs. I knew about where some of the favorite nesting areas were, but there was always one or two old hens who could hide their nests so cleverly that it would take a Scotland Yard detective to find them. And when we started running short on eggs, we knew that there were some hidden nests we hadn't found.

Frequently, I would find a hen already settin' on her eggs, and it was necessary to reach under her and retrieve the shelled treasures. That's when the battle began!

If you've never been pecked on the hand by a settin' hen, you don't know what fury is! And if you think an old settin' hen is going to give up her eggs without a fight, you've got another thought (or peck) coming!

But I always had some extra motivation to hang in there — because I knew that my only hope to get some candy when the rolling store came around was to find some extra eggs to trade. Or come up with a dime to go to the movies. So I always eventually got the eggs, when I could find them. But of course, we never did find all the nests in time.

And one pretty spring morning an old Dominecker hen would come strutting proudly across the yard, clucking authoritatively to a toddling brood of baby chicks. Then we knew that we had unintentionally traded some eggs for a new bunch of chickens!

Kids of today will never know what it is to steal an egg or two out from under an old hen who doesn't want to let it go. But you've made up your mind you're gonna see that Saturday picture show!

Funeral Home Fans

One of the hottest places I know of in the summertime is a country church house packed full of people.

Air conditioning was unheard of back in the good ole days when I was growing up. Well, at least, air conditioning as we know it today.

Back then, however, we had individual air conditioners for each member of the congregation. We called them funeral home fans.

The cardboard fan was a familiar fixture on the pews in every country church; and a church service, singing or funeral on a hot summer day was a frenzy of fanning and sweat-wiping all over the house.

The reason we called them funeral home fans was that they were donated by a commercial concern whose name and advertising message were printed on the back. And the usual donor was the local funeral home, though other business firms also did this.

The other side of the fan, made of stiff cardboard with a flimsy wood handle attached, always had a pretty color picture on it. So if things got a little dull we could always stop fanning long enough to look at the picture and read the advertising message. And that's what the sponsor was hoping for.

A young man who brought his favorite girl to the service, or the singing, could show his love and devotion to her by fanning her. This also gave him a good excuse to sit extra close to her, too!

It was interesting just to observe the audience at a singing, because they waved their fans almost in unison with the time of the music, with occasional departures to swat at a persistent fly or gnat.

When mechanical air conditioning came along, the cardboard fan suffered a gradual demise. But somebody told me recently that such fans are still given away in some areas.

It would sure save a lot of expensive electricity in these modern times to let each person do his own fanning. But one drawback would remain: how to keep your shirt or britches from sticking to the back or seats of those pine pews as the sweat soaked through!

129

Brush Arbors

How long has it been since you've seen a brush arbor?

I haven't seen one in many years, but this used to be a common sight in every rural community in summertime.

Now, for you young folks or city slickers who don't know what I'm talking about, a brush arbor was a shelter made of brush under which revival meetings were held in the rural areas during the summer.

A brush arbor was constructed by clearing off a place in a patch of woods alongside a road, by cutting poles and sinking them in the ground, running cross poles over them about eight or ten feet high, then by covering the structure with brush. Sometimes standing trees were used for the corner supports of the brush top.

It really wasn't tight enough to keep out much rain, but it did shield out the hot sun during the daytime.

Some country churches owe their beginning to a small meeting held in a brush arbor.

And in other cases the brush arbor meeting was the old timey version of today's community-wide worship services where people of the different denominations get together for special services.

By the time a brush arbor went through the winter it was dried out and useless without being renovated. But anyway, it was normally just a temporary structure designed for one-time use or a short period of service.

There were always some traveling evangelists who carried their services into local communities aside from individual church sponsorship, and the brush arbor was frequently used for such meetings, just as tents are today.

It worked pretty well, except for times when a quick rain came up in the middle of the service.

Now the brush arbor has faded from the scene, along with ox yokes, grasshopper stocks, shoe lasts and old oaken buckets.

But for everyone who has ever attended a shouting and singing meeting under one, the old brush arbor —though gone — will never be forgotten!

Good Ole Days' Prices

I seldom go into a store and buy a candy bar, but the other day I decided to pamper my sweet tooth a little bit and so I shopped around at the candy counter in a supermarket.

I got to looking at the fifty cent candy bars and reflecting on the fact that they were less than half the size that the same sort of candy bars used to be when they sold for a nickel when I was a boy. Of course, to be perfectly honest, I would have to admit that fifty cents today is much easier for me to come by than a nickel when I was a boy!

Back then, I can remember when men worked 12 and 14 hour days on the farm, at a sawmill, or in other hard jobs for as little as 50 cents a day. During the Depression days they were anxious to get work at any price, just to keep some bread on the family table.

And that fifty cents would go a long way in buying food back then. The other day I ran across a list of grocery prices published in an ad by a big food chain in 1932. Read some of these prices and weep:

Bacon, 15 cents a pound; eggs, 18 cents a dozen; Ivory soap, 5 bars for 23 cents; butter, 2 pounds for 41 cents; large loaf of rye bread, 7 cents.

So far as food is concerned, though, it is still a better buy today, comparatively speaking, than it was back then. In other words, the average wage earner spends a much smaller percentage of his pay to buy food for his family than he did half a century ago. And the average family eats much better today than was the case back then.

Those were the days when a new pair of shoes cost $2, a new suit cost $5, and a new car cost $500.

Going a few years on further back: one reader sent me a copy of a bill of sale for a 1917 Model T Ford touring car which his grandfather purchased on December 1, 1917. The bill of sale lists the base price of the car at $360, then adds $9.46 for war tax, $2.70 for 10 gallons of gas, 75 cents for a gallon of oil, and freight charges of $37.50.

To young folks today, these prices seem unreal. But they are recent enough to be remembered by many people who are still living.

There's no doubt about it. The dollar just doesn't do as much for us nowdays as it used to. But on the other hand, not many folks will do as much for the dollar as they used to, either!

Local Philosophers

In my rounds recently, I stopped by a country store to get "a big orange" and visit a spell with some of the local philosophers who were leaning back in their cane bottom chairs and discussing the changing times.

One fellow said he could remember when his mother used to gather up all their dirty clothes every week, tie them up in a sheet, put them in a homemade truck wagon and head for the spring down on their farm to wash them.

"She would also carry a big jug of buttermilk in the wagon and leave it cooling in the spring water while she washed clothes. When she got home, the cold buttermilk was sure good with a big pone of cornbread cooked in the old wood burning stove and some turnip greens cooked in an old iron pot," he added.

And, speaking of good ole timey eating, another fellow let me in on an old recipe for a mouth-watering breakfast which was a favorite with his family:

Take salt pork and make your favorite batter for frying fish, along with one egg. Simmer the pork in water in a skillet for 5 to 10 minutes, pour off the water, take out the pork and batter it, then fry it like fish until it is browned.

He allowed that the thin gravy you get from frying the pork is out of this world with biscuits and sorghum.

Another fellow got to talking about cat holes everybody used to have in their kitchen door.

He explained that with these the cat was free to come in and go out at his or her pleasure.

This reminded me of one man who had three cat holes in his kitchen door. When asked why, he said, "When I say scat, I mean scat!"

Cats were much more than pets to us back in those days. We depended upon them to keep down the population of rats and mice around the household and the farm.

We always had a big bunch of cats at our place, and we even had a special place to feed them which we called "the cat porch." It was a little porch attached to the side of the house by the back door just outside the kitchen.

My favorite thing about the cat porch was, however, the fact that this was where we always made ice cream on Saturday nights in the summertime and on the Fourth of July!

Log Cabins

All over the country there's a revival of interest in log houses these days, as lots of people are choosing to build new homes with some of the same thoughts of sturdiness as the old log cabins of our early history.

In fact, many of these old log cabins still exist, mostly in museums and parks. After 100 years or more, they're likely to be just as strong and sturdy as when they were built.

I was born and raised in the same house which my daddy was born and raised in, a log house which was built by my grandfather when he settled our old home place just after the Civil War.

Folks in those days didn't move around nearly as much as they do now, and it was not unusual for several generations of a family to live at the "old home place."

In those days nobody even thought of going to the hospital to have a baby. Babies were born right there at home, and unless there were complications of some kind they were usually delivered by a local woman who was the midwife of the community, with no doctor present.

Midwives played a prominent role in local communities in those days, even in the towns and cities. It was a necessity with us out in the country. But for many folks in town — even some well-to-do families —having one's baby in the home with just a midwife assisting was the custom.

Well, by the time I came along our old log cabin didn't look like one from the outside, because my daddy had fancied it up by putting weather boarding on the outside and replacing the wood shingle roof with a tin

roof. But inside, the logs were still exposed, bearing the marks of where they were hewn with an ax, and notched together at the ends, with not a nail in them to hold them together.

Tighter flooring had been put down over the original plank floor. And so, even though the wind whipped in pretty strong on a windy day, it was nothing like the original log cabins, where you would wake up on a cold winter morning and find snow on your bed covers — and where you could throw a cat between the cracks in the floor!

Now, as I travel around and see the fine houses which people live in, I am so thankful that we have good housing today.

We didn't know any better then, but it surely would be traumatic today for most of us to have to go back to our log cabins and rickety shacks after having lived in today's comfortable dwellings.

The Family Trunk

Recently I was visiting some friends of mine in their home, and they took me to a back room, opened up an old family trunk and began to show me some of the prized keepsakes from their family back through several generations.

As I looked at some of these priceless collectibles from their family history, I was remembering that back in the good ole days, just about every family had such a trunk in which they stored keepsakes from previous generations as well as current family treasures.

The old family trunk was the early day version of the foot locker, which is still a popular item for youngsters going away to college. Back then, it was made of thin wood, reinforced with metal bands, and usually had some fancy designs on it. The top was rounded over in convex fashion so it could hold more. The trunk was where we stored quilts and clothes. And it was also where we kept family mementos and valuable papers.

I can still remember how as a boy I loved to rummage through my grandma's old trunk. She had been dead for many years, but in her trunk — which had been carefully preserved — I could find some of her old clay pipes which she used to smoke, and even some of the old letters she had received from various friends and members of the family. There were tintypes of my daddy when he was a boy, and of other members of the family from bygone days.

There was a lot of history there, including family history and records which have now been carelessly lost and can never be replaced.

139

Every once in awhile I run across someone who still has an old family trunk full of such gems, and sometimes folks share some of this fascinating memorabilla with me.

It is regrettable that in these fast paced times, fewer and fewer of us take the time to keep these things so that we may someday reflect back on pleasant memories, or that future generations in our families may have more things to remember their ancestors by.

I see in people today a renewed interest in and affection for many of these things from the old days. This is reflected in the lively interest today in antiques, and even in such hobbies as collecting old bottles.

This age of disposables, of intangibles, of constant moving about, has left in people a longing for the old stable values, the roots in living.

Maybe it would be a good thing if the old family trunk came back in style. Or at least, each family could devise its own method of housing family archives so they might be safely kept for the years to come!

Pulling Fodder

When I travel around the countryside during the summertime, my mouth waters when I see that tall green corn growing in the fields and gardens. Because I savor those delicious fresh-from-the-stalk roastnears, (which some fancy-talking folks insist on calling "roasting ears").

But as long as I live, I suppose I will never escape the thought of what an awful job it was to pull fodder in such corn fields toward the latter part of the summer.

My daddy always thought it was a terrible waste of feed not to pull the fodder blades off the corn about the time the ears got mature and the blades began to get a slight tinge of brown around the edges.

There never was a hotter job devised by man than pulling fodder on a hot summer day! Not a breeze hits you down between those rows of cornstalks. And the edges of the blades scratch and rasp at your hot sweaty skin something fierce!

The fodder is pulled and put together in "hands." A "hand" is the amount of fodder one can hold in his hand. Each "hand" of fodder is tied with a few blades of fodder and lodged on the top of a broken stalk to dry in the sun for a few hours. Then, the next step is to group about four "hands" of fodder together to make a bundle, which is also tied with some strips of fodder pressed together.

Late in the afternoon, after the fodder has cured in the hot sun all day, it's time to come around with the wagon and load up all the fodder to haul it to the barn. But even then, the still-green fodder can't be put away into storage until it has been spread out to dry in the sun for another day, to make sure it won't heat up after it is stacked in the crib.

The only other job I can think of that was worse than pulling fodder was picking velvet beans. Used to, farmers would plant velvet beans in their corn, so that they could have an extra crop of feed for the livestock to harvest after the corn was laid by.

Velvet beans made good cattle feed, but they had stinging fuzz on them that was as bad as okra. And after a day in the hot corn field picking velvet beans, there was no way to estimate the total amount of misery one had endured!

Sometimes I used to wonder if my daddy was bordering on child abuse by making us pick those horrible things!

It's been a long time since I have seen any velvet beans growing in a corn field. And I had just as soon never see any again!

Pulling fodder and picking velvet beans are two of my least favorite memories from the good ole days. And I'm thankful that today's generations don't have to be subjected to such cruel and unusual punishment!

Chopping Cotton

I got out my trusty hoe the other day to work around my young dogwood trees. And while I was getting rid of some of the pesky weeds and grass with that hoe, some unpleasant memories began to surface about all the time I used to spend on the business end of a hoe when cotton chopping time arrived.

One of the least favorites of all the things I had to do was chop cotton. It ranked right along there with such other jobs as milking cows and pulling fodder. But like the other tasks, it had to be done. And there was no use arguing or even thinking otherwise.

I was always amazed at how you could plow the ground real good and get it real clean and then plant nothing but cottonseed, but by the time the cotton came up, for every stalk of cotton there were a dozen sprigs of grass!

Another amazing thing was how close to the cotton the grass liked to grow. Why, it looked like that grass just loved the little cotton and wanted to snuggle up to it!

So, it was a tedious task to chop away the grass without also chopping down the young tender cotton stalks, especially when there were two or three rocks or sticks right here in the way.

And you talk about patience! You don't know what patience means until you spend two or three hard hours working your way with a hoe down a row of cotton, then stop and look around and see that you're still a long way from the end of that row. Even worse, you see hundreds more rows across the field yet to be chopped!

And it wasn't much consolation to wake up on Saturday morning and hear rain falling on the tin roof, meaning that it would be too wet to chop cotton that day. Because my daddy always had plenty of jobs waiting for those rainy days, like shucking and shelling corn in the barn.

Ironically, it was not the demise of cotton as our exclusive money crop that relieved the younger generation from the terrible job of hoeing cotton. Herbicides were developed several years ago which eliminated the need for hand hoeing to control weeds and grass.

But all that fancy stuff came entirely too late to save me from such drudgery! Oh well! I guess that's just the way the clod crumbles!

Cotton Pickin' Days

One of the worst things about growing up on a small farm in the fall of the year was that every afternoon as soon as we got home from school, we had to grab our canvas pick sacks, head for the cotton patch and pick cotton till sundown.

But one of the best things about it was, if we could pick a wagon load of cotton during the week, we'd get to take it to town to the gin on Saturday.

We lived eight miles out in the country on rough, hilly country roads. It took several hours to get to town in a wagon. So we didn't get to go to town very often. However, when we did get to go, it was quite a treat!

Thus, the anticipation of taking a bale of cotton to the gin on Saturday gave us considerable motivation to work hard all week to "get a bale out." The sideboards were put on the two-horse wagon early Monday morning, with the goal of picking about 1500 pounds of loose cotton to hopefully turn out a 500 pound bale when it was ginned.

As the week wore on, it seemed like we'd never fill that big ole wagon with cotton! Some days we would work til pitch dark to grab a few extra pick sacks full. But with a little luck we'd have it rounded up to the top of the sideboards by quitting time on Friday. So Daddy would say: "Ok, we'll get it to the gin tomorrow."

On Saturday morning it was no trouble to get us kids out of bed before daylight, so we could get ourselves and the horses or mules fed, hitch up the wagon and be on the road before the sun came up. If it was a chilly morning, I'd sometimes dig out a "burrowing hole" in the loose cotton and get down in it to stay warm on the way to the gin.

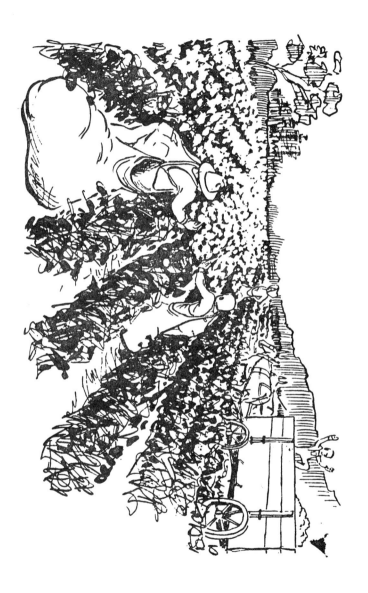

We always hoped to arrive at the gin yard ahead of most of the other farmers, so we wouldn't have to wait in line so long. Usually, though, it was on towards dinnertime before our turn came. But that was ok because there was plenty to entertain us as we watched the ginning activity and visited with all the other folks who were waiting too.

Besides, the biggest treat of all was getting to eat a bought lunch. Usually we ate sardines and crackers from the nearby store, and perhaps some cheese carved off a big hoop of cheese on the bottom of an upturned barrel there in the little store. If cotton prices were pretty good, we sometimes got dessert too — an ice cream cone or candy bar. And maybe even an RC Cola and Moon Pie.

Finally we were ready to drive the wagon up under the gin shed. And I just loved to watch as a gin worker would maneuver that big suction tube to pull the cotton out of the wagon bed and into the gin.

The hum of that bodacious cotton gin was really something! And I delighted in watching through the glass as the cotton moved through the gin saws, with the lint falling into the big bale press and the seed into a special hopper.

After the wagon had been emptied, Daddy would pull it aside and hitch the mules while we watched the big press work, with the gin hands putting the burlap covering and steel bands around the compressed bale — which was finally spit out onto the scales — after a sharp knife had been used to slash the burlap and pull out a bale sample for the buyers.

We waited breathlessly to see if we'd achieved that 500 pound bale we were striving for. And of course Daddy was anxious to get the word from the cotton buyer on how much money the bale would bring.

Finally the transaction was completed, Daddy had some money in his overall pockets and we headed for home with a partial wagon load of cottonseed to feed the cows.

Another fall day, full of excitement and adventure! Time to think about starting all over again on Monday!

Wagons

Long before the days of cars and trucks, wagons and buggies were our chief means of transportation. And lots of folks who had bought cars and trucks before the Great Depression hit had to park them and go back to their wagons for many years, because they simply couldn't afford to operate these motor vehicles anymore. Car sheds were full of vehicles that sat jacked up on blocks (to keep the tires from rotting) while wagons became the chief means of transportation again.

The wagon was one of the greatest inventions ever, and it served many generations well. During the week it was used to haul fertilizer and other supplies, bring the crops from the fields during harvest time and haul wood in the wintertime.

On Sunday, it took the family to church. And occasionally it took them to town.

Some of the wagon manufacturers got into the business of making automobiles and tractors, as these mechanized vehicles came along. But many of them continued to make wagons as their primary product for many years.

Few younger people today have ever seen a wagon like those we used to have, unless they've seen an antique wagon in a parade. It was truly a marvelous and ingenious piece of equipment!

There were one-horse and two-horse versions, depending upon the size and use for which the particular models were designed. The two-horse models, of course, were much larger and heavier and could carry bigger loads.

The horses or mules were hitched to singletrees at the front of the wagon, with a long tongue between them.

This tongue, (like about a three-inch square piece of timber), was connected to the front axle, which was attached to the underside of the wagon bed on a turning radius device so the front wheels would turn from side to side as the driver guided his steeds — much like the steering mechanisms on automobiles or trailers.

The rear axle was connected by the coupling pole, another strong piece of timber which ran from the front, underneath the wagon bed, on through the rear axle and out the back for a couple of feet, for extra strength and stability.

This latter device provided a favorite activity for us kids, as we would sometimes be allowed to hitch a ride on the coupling pole on the way to and from the fields or woods.

The driver sat on a board laid across the top of the wagon bed sides at the front, dangling his legs down in front of the bed. But for those trips to church or town, or when more confort and style were called for, a wagon seat mounted on springs was placed at the front of the bed so that two or three people could sit in it more comfortably.

The brakes consisted of another piece of timber attached underneath the bed, with brake shoes protruding out just in front of the rear wheels. They were spring-mounted or slide-mounted, so that the driver could apply them to the wheels by pulling on a rope attached to a vertical pole.

The heavy wood wheels had steel rims. And when the rims would start getting loose, all it took to tighten them was to take the wheel off and soak it in water for a day or so.

Axle grease was applied regularly to the spindles of the ends of the axles, so that the wheels would turn freely on their massive hubs. If a wheel started squeaking, it was immediately greased. (Thus the saying: "A squeaking wheel gets the grease").

Yes, the wagon served us well for many generations. I remember it with much affection and appreciation!

Ground Slides

The other day I got to thinking about ground slides, and realized that probably most people today have never seen a ground slide, and have no idea what it is.

Back in the Depression days when I was growing up most families could not afford a truck, and many of us could not even afford a good wagon. And so we reverted back to the old homemade ground slide which had been a slow but reliable transportation vehicle many generations before.

We used the ground slide not only to haul corn to the mill, but for many other transporting jobs around the place, such as bringing corn and cotton in from the field to the barn or crib. And in dry weather, when our well went dry, we hauled drinking water from a nearby spring in big barrels on a ground slide.

Maybe I'd better explain what a ground slide is, for the benefit of some of you city folks.

It is a rectangular platform something like four feet wide by six feet long, made of heavy boards, with runners underneath on both sides made out of two by six boards stood on edge with the front ends beveled off.

The slide is pulled by horse or mule by means of a singletree which is attached to the front end of the runners.

When properly made, a ground slide glides along the ground fairly easily, and a horse or mule can pull a heavy load on one.

During the Depression, many farmers were too poor to afford a farm wagon so they made ground slides to haul things on.

I've hauled a many of a load of fertilizer to the field on a ground slide, then put it out by hand with a guano horn. I'll bet many of you don't know what a guano horn is.

Before the days of mule-drawn fertilizer distributors, (or "fertilizer knockers," as we called them), folks put out fertilizer by hand with guano horns.

The guano horn was so named because it was a long cylindrical gadget made of tin and about a couple of inches in diameter, with a funnel-shaped top resembling the flared bell of a trumpet or other horn.

To put out fertilizer, you walked along the row with a knapsack filled with fertilizer, feeding the "guano" a handful at a time into the horn and letting it drop in a directed path down onto the row.

Ground slides, guano horns, singletrees and other such pieces of equipment are long since relics of the past. But for those of us who used them, they're gone but not forgotten!

New Shoes

One thing I used to always look forward to in the spring of the year was getting a new pair of shoes.

Along toward the end of winter, when it was nearly time to start plowing, my daddy would take me to town to get fitted for a new pair of plow shoes.

I can still remember how good that new leather smelled! It was clean, soft and pliable, and felt so good on my feet.

The shoes were high top brogans, with shinny hooks instead of the top three eyes for the strings to catch on.

I was always so proud of my new shoes that I would save them from the fields as long as possible, wearing them with my clean overalls to Sunday school at least a time or two before I had to start plowing with them on.

Once I wore them to the field, they were marred and dirty from then on, because there's no way to walk behind a steel beam plow in fresh-turned dirt without messing up your shoes on the outside and getting them full of dirt on the inside.

Of course, as soon as the weather got hot we mostly went barefooted all summer long. I can still remember how tender the bottoms of my feet were the first few days, with every sharp rock hurting something awful. But by the time summer was halfway gone the bottoms of my feet were so toughened that I could practically walk on a piece of barbed wire without hurting them.

Those of you who have gone barefooted a lot know too that one of the most painful things in the world is a stone bruise. You get it when you step down real hard on a rock and inflict a deep bruise in the bottom of your foot. The injured tissue goes real deep, turns purple, and takes a long time to heal.

Another hazard to summertime barefootedness is stepping on a bee. Not many children have escaped that one!

On well, I suppose for most people in these affluent times we now live in, getting a new pair of shoes is not much of an event.

But for those of us who grew up in the country in Depression times, that new $1.98 pair of shoes we got once a year was something to look forward to with much anticipation.

Come to think of it, most of us might still get pretty excited if we discovered shoes at that price in the store today!

Picking Blackberries

When spring rolls around every year, I start keeping an eye out for all the wild blackberries I can find growing around my neck of the woods. And when that late cold snap comes around the first of June, I know that it's "Blackberry Winter," which means the blackberries are blooming and "good eatin' time" is just around the corner!

When I was growing up, I never knew you could pick blackberries with anything but a syrup bucket. By hanging the pail over the upper corner of the bib of your overalls, then fastening the gallus back, both hands are free to part the vines and pick the berries.

We always picked blackberries after a shower, when it was too wet to plow or to hoe cotton.

Now, as everybody knows, blackberries grow in hard-to-get-at places, and they seem to actually reach out to attack you with their sharp briars when you approach their glossy black fruit to pick them.

Furthermore, the wet grass and vines after a summer shower seem to delight the chiggers or redbugs, who have a feast on the blackberry pickers. It doesn't take long for those itchy red bumps to start appearing all over the body!

Yet, when you head home with your syrup bucket rounded up full of fat, juicy blackberries, you know it's all been worthwhile, because there are few things in this world more heavenly than a big blackberry cobbler.

You make it in a deep enameled pan, with a generous filling of fresh blackberries and sugar and plenty of homemade biscuit dumplings. Cook it down real good, until the sweetened blackberry juice begins to thicken and the dumplings start to get brown across the top.

Then, you're ready for the feast! Get the biggest dinner plate you can find and prop up one side of it with a case knife so the juice won't run everywhere when you pile that hot pie on your plate.

Once you get a double-sized helping of cobbler on your plate, put a big hunk of fresh-churned country butter right smack on top of it and let it melt and run down and mix with the juice.

First thing you know, your palate will feel even better than the rest of you feels when you get to scratching those chigger bites!

Seems like we have a special "week" set aside for just about everything these days. Wonder why we don't have a "Blackberry Week" to celebrate the joys of picking blackberries, scratching chigger bites, and tanking up on hot buttered blackberry cobbler?

Come to think of it, though, a week wouldn't be long enough. A whole month would be more like it!

Chewing Sugar Cane

If you didn't have the privilege of growing up on the farm back in the good ole days, you don't really and truly know what good eatin' sure 'nuff is!

We country kids knew nothing about "fast foods" or other modern store-bought delights. But we had all sorts of mouth-watering delights that tasted mighty good to us.

One of my favorite things in the late summer and early fall was chewing sugar cane.

My daddy always picked out a good spot for the cane patch — a low place where there was rich sandy loam soil and plenty of moisture.

In the spring we plowed furrows and carefully covered the stalks of seed cane, saved from the previous season by covering them with sawdust or straw in the potato house out by the barn.

(Some of you may not know that sugar cane reproduces not from seed but from nodules or buds which grow in each joint of the stalk.)

The cane was carefully tended with hoe and plow through the growing season, so by late summer we had fat tall blue stalks of sugar cane ready for chewing.

I could hardly wait for Sunday afternoon to come, when we kids would head for the cane patch with our pocket knives to cut and chew sugar cane.

First you find the biggest stalk, then carefully strip the fodder, being careful not to cut your hands on the sawtooth edges. Then you cut the stalk at the ground, top it at the first blue area at the top of the stalk, and the feast begins.

The sweetest part is at the bottom, so we were always taught to chew the top joints first, thus having the sweeter and juicier morsels to look forward to.

The knotty joint is cut off, then with a sharp knife a ring is cut around and through the thick bark just above the next joint below, so the blue bark can be peeled off in strips, leaving the white inner stalk just oozing with sugary juice.

What a taste treat as you chomp down on the juicy cane and swallow the juice, then spit out the pulp and go again!

It seemed like a shame to make such a delicacy into syrup, though it had to be harvested and made before frost. As every cane connoisseur knows, frostbitten sugar cane has a terrible off-flavor.

Of course, once it is made into ribbon cane syrup, it becomes a totally new delight when generously applied on hot buttered biscuits on brisk fall mornings.

The way you eat ribbon cane syrup is to heat it on top of the stove before you put it on the table. Then you take a big dinner plate and prop it up on one side with a case knife and plop a big glob of butter on the lower side of the plate. Pour the hot syrup over the butter and stir it while it melts to mix the butter with the syrup.

Then you take a homemade biscuit and sop it in the buttered syrup. And just do what comes naturally. I guarantee a larrapin delight! (Sorghum works the same way, except that it isn't as good to chew from the stalk out in the field or at the mill).

Just make sure you have several biscuits ready. One won't be near enough!

Making Syrup

Syrup-making time always meant a lot of hard work for me when I was growing up on the farm.

It meant working in the hot field stripping the cane, cutting it and hauling it to the mill, then feeding the cane into the mill while a plodding old mule walked round and round pulling a long pole to turn the mill rollers to squeeze out the juice.

It meant keeping the fire going under the big pan while the syrup maker cooked down the juice, then helping fill the syrup buckets and finally hauling the syrup home in the wagon.

But there were a lot of fun things about making syrup too. Like drinking some of the fresh juice out of a tin dipper before it ran into the pan. Tasting the hot syrup fresh out of the cooking pan, before it went into the buckets. And savoring the sights and sounds and smells that are unique to syrup mills.

One thing that I miss about modern syrup mills is the smoke and odor of the burning pummies. Unfortunately modern air pollution regulations have made it necessary for the syrup makers to dispose of their discarded cane stalks in other ways. So the gushy white smoke and the distinctive odor of burning cane pummies is no longer found around syrup mills.

In fact, even the syrup mills themselves are largely gone in most areas. The old syrup makers have mostly retired or died, and not many young people are taking up this art. Besides, the shortage of hand labor on farms today has caused many farmers who used to grow cane for syrup to give it up altogether.

I suppose that syrup making, like most other things, is inevitably moving toward mechanization and modernization in all its processes, from the farm to the market.

Fortunately, we still have a few ole timey syrup mills left. And the stuff they turn out is guaranteed to make a hot buttered biscuit into food fit for a king!

Oh yes! That was the final reward for those long hot days of labor at syrup making time.

A plateful of hot syrup with plenty of fresh country butter melted in it, and a panful of hot biscuits for sopping. No king ever had any food better than that I'm sure!

The Old Farm Shop

One of my favorite places to be on a cold winter day back in the good ole days was puttering around the shop. A cluttered farm shop was a relaxing place on such a day, especially if it was raining outside and too bad to work out of doors.

This time of year, the work wasn't usually so pressing as it would be later, as spring plowing time neared. Then, there would be plow points to be sharpened, singletrees to be fixed, planter parts to be mended.

But as for now, the crops were pretty well in and it was a few months yet until time to plant again, so a fellow could more comfortably piddle with lots of little things that needed doing. Like repairing the wagon tongue or putting some new brake shoes on the buggy, making a new handle for Mama's best butcher knife, or even building the kids a new truck wagon for Christmas.

In fact, if the weather was real bad outside and a fellow had a good fire going in the rusty old stove there in the shop, a man sort of felt justified just to sit by the heater and pore over the Sears Roebuck catalog and catch up on the farm magazines.

The farm shop wasn't a good example of housekeeping. Old, torn horse blankets and broken horse collars hung from wooden pegs or rusty nails; broken plowstocks leaned against the walls; shop corners were crowded with shovels, spades, sledge hammers and crow bars, pitchforks with broken handles. A half used bag of phosphate added its fragrance to burlap bags, half-empty cans of paint, a pile of lumber beneath the bench.

The old forge, where coal was burned to heat metal for pounding into various shapes and forms and objects, was black and rusty. There was at least a couple of inches of dust covering the massive iron anvil anchored on the top of a heavy piece of sweetgum log.

The dirt floor was damp and musty, mingling with the smells of rusting iron, coal dust and mildewed leather.

Old fashioned farm shops such as I knew as a boy are gone now. Today the shop resembles a garage with intricate machinery waiting for its winter overhaul.

But many of us still remember the farm shop of yesteryear and the pleasant hours spent there catching up on odd jobs.

Or just relaxing while cold winter winds whistled under the eaves and icy rain played tic-tac against cobweb-blotched windows. And while green oak and hickory wood made cheerful music in an old pot bellied stove.

Cow Personalties

Everybody who grew up on a farm and kept milk cows knows how it is with a bunch of cows when springtime arrives each year.

All winter long they've been standing at the gap between the pasture and the barn every evening a long time before sundown, ready to be let in to the barn lot and into their respective stalls to be fed and milked.

But now, spring has come. The pastures have turned green, the grass is young and tender and tasty, and the cantankerous old cows just won't come to the barn when it's milking time. So, it was always my job to go to the pasture and round them up and drive them home.

When we had a cow that was expecting a calf, we always had to watch out for her. Sure enough, one afternoon she would turn up missing, and we knew she was hidden out somewhere down in the pasture with that new baby calf.

So I'd head out to the pasture to look for her and her baby, which she would have hidden somewhere in a clump of bushes or a briar patch. She'd hear me coming and get as still as she could, so she wouldn't make that cowbell around her neck tingle and give away her hiding place.

If she was an especially crafty old coot, sometimes dark would nearly catch me before I located her, picked up the little calf in my arms and headed for home, with the proud and concerned mother tagging close behind.

Another bad happening this time of year with our cows occurred when the bitterweeds began to grow. Our pasture had lots of bitterweeds in it, and for some strange reason our old cows would sometime take a spell of eating those foul-tasting plants.

We always knew it at the supper table. Because after milking time, when we poured the milk and started to drink it, it had such a bitter taste that it was un-drinkable.

Another thing all you cow milkers will remember is how when the cockle burs began to grow every spring, they seemed to be attracted to cows' tails like metal to a magnet. And friends, until you've been hit on the side of the head by a wet cow's tail matted with cockle burs, you haven't really lived!

Oh well, I could write an entire book about all my country boy experiences with cows. I doubt if it'd sell, though. Those who haven't been through it wouldn't know a thing I was talking about. And those who had would sure want to forget!

Picture Taking

Being a camera buff, I enjoy browsing around the camera departments in big stores and ogling over the new models that the camera makers are marketing these days.

My mind gets boggled in a hurry when I see and read about all the automatic features they're building into picture-making machines.

About all one has to do is point the camera at the subject and say "when" by pressing a button. The camera focuses itself, sets the proper lens opening according to the light conditions, takes the picture and then winds itself to get ready for the next shot.

Needless to say, it fusses at you if you don't do something right — by blinking at you, making a noise or otherwise taking steps to make sure your picture will turn out just right.

And, of course, it also comes with or can be equipped with a fancy electronic flash attachment (or has one built in) that throws just the right amount of light on the subject at a speed of 1/2000 of a second.

Naturally, you can use a variety of lenses that will do all kinds of magic things to the camera's eye — like telescoping way out to pull a subject far away practically to arm's length. Or stretching the range of vision several times as wide as a normal lens can see.

Truth is, some of these fancy cameras are miniature computers designed to take pictures — with film that is sometimes so "fast" that it can record images practically in the dark. Indeed, there are infrared cameras today that can literally take pictures in the dark!

Shucks! I'm beginning to long for the good ole days of the famous Brownie box camera! How many of you remember the Brownie? It was basically just a little wood box less than half as big as a bread basket. There was a good-sized round hole in the middle of the front of the box. That was the lens. On the top left front corner of the box there was a small square hole, which you looked through to snap the picture. That was the viewfinder. The roll of film was wound on reels inside the box.

And that was about it. All you had to do to make a picture was to stand somebody in front of a bush or car or the side of the house — in the sun — and snap the shutter. Just get far enough back to get them in the viewfinder square, and that was it! Sometimes the picture was a mite fuzzy, but otherwise it was pretty good.

Well, I never heard of anybody getting ulcers back in those days trying to figure how to take pictures with their "Kodak." Like I'm about to get trying to figure out how to work the fancy new camera I broke down and bought the other day.

I've also found out, to my dismay, that I look just as ugly in the pictures made by the fancy new computerized automatic camera as I did in the snapshots made by the old Brownie. Besides that, a roll of film for the new one costs more than the Brownie itself did back then.

Oh well. Our old Brownie finally quit after about 30 years of picture making. And after the mule stepped on it.

Maybe my new one will last that long. That should give me enough time to figure out how to use it!

Foot Logs

This piece is a story of adventure, thrills and great perils. No, it's not a mystery story or a science fiction tale. It's recollections about walking across foot logs over creeks, branches, small streams and big ditches.

For you uninitiated, a foot log was simply a log laid across a creek or ditch for folks to walk across on. I'm sure the Indians must have used them first in this country, before there was such a thing as a bridge. But when I was a boy they were still a necessary and integral part of country life.

In fact, bridges were a rarity even on public roads until automobiles became commonplace. Instead of crossing streams on a bridge, folks just forded the streams at shallow points. This was possible on horseback and in wagons, and even in the early cars with their high wheels.

So foot logs were a convenience, to enable one to cross a steam without having to wade through it.

We had a small creek cutting across our pasture bottom which almost always flooded every time there was a big rain. When this happened, it would catch our cows on the other side of the creek from home, and they would be afraid to cross the creek. So it fell my lot to go and drive them across.

A foot log enabled us to cross the creek even at flood stage. And when there were young calves in the herd that were too small to swim across the creek, I would pick them up and carry them across on the foot log while the concerned mother cows swam alongside.

Folks, if you've never negotiated a foot log across a raging creek carrying a wiggling calf in your arms, you've really missed something!

172

Now and then, on a much-traveled path, folks would construct foot bridges, complete with banisters or handrails along the sides. But a plain old foot log was the norm around our neck of the woods, with the top not even trimmed or flattened.

I've fallen off of lots of foot logs in my day, including several times with my Sunday clothes on. And I've done my share of fording streams as well.

That's why I have such a warm appreciation for nice high, wide, dry bridges!

Fighting Flies

We've been hearing a lot lately about all those aerosol sprays we are using, and how they may be messing up our atmosphere. That's one of those modern things that we never even imagined back in the good ole days.

Not only were such things as hair spray unhead of back then, but we never knew much about any kind of insecticides. Certainly, we never thought about any kind of spray for flying insects.

"What has four wheels and flies?," goes a modern riddle. The answer is, of course, "a garbage truck!" Well, when I was growing up we could have easily paraphrased it thusly: "What has four legs and flies?" The answer would have been: "The dinner table."

Flies were a constant in-the-house summer companion in those days before air conditioning and not-so-good window screens.

Every time we sat down to eat, the flies were right there with us. During everyday meals with the family, we just waved at the pesky critters now and then to sort of keep them shooed away from our food.

But when company came, we were a little more fastidious. One person was usually stationed by the table to wave a peach limb to keep the flies run off from the food while everybody else ate.

The only other weapon we had in our battle with flies in those days was sticky fly paper. Remember that stuff? It came in a small round cardboard container about the size of a snuff box. You opened it and out dangled a long strip of paper with the stickiest surface you ever saw. Any fly that happened to touch this was caught and trapped. Sometimes it came in sheets, which were laid on the table to catch unwary flies.

I got to searching some stores here awhile back to see whether or not this sticky fly paper is still available. Sure enough, I found some.

I hope it works a whole lot better than one of those fancy electronic "fly and insect zappers" that I tried a few years ago on my patio. Indeed, it zapped a few flying insects. But most of them just ignored it or just seemed to use it to light their way straight to the food on the table!

Back to the matter of peach limbs: Another common use which my mother made of peach limbs was for a "hickory." With the leaves stripped off, the supple young limbs applied vigorously to the bare legs of a disobedient child did more to straighten him out than all of today's modern psychiatry put together!

Kudzu

Back on our old home place we used to have a hillside where the trees had been cut away years before for timber and we never did figure out how to grow anything on it.

This particular spot had old poor hard soil and would hardly grow decent bitterweeds, much less pasture grass or crops. So we just sort of gave up on it and let it gradually begin to wash away.

But then one day the county agent told us about a new plant called kudzu, which he said would grow just about anywhere. He said it would cover that ground and keep it from eroding, and it would be good for grazing and hay.

He knew where we could get some kudzu crowns (roots) to set out on that hillside, and he assured us that it would take root and grow rapidly.

Boy, did he made an understatement there! Not only did it take root and grow rapidly, but it took off like a freight train going down a steep grade! Before I wore out my new overalls, it had covered not only that spot but had started covering up several trees along the edge of the field. Not to mention all the old rusting plowstocks lying around the place!

Thousands of farmers like us latched on to kudzu as a soil-holding plant that animals loved to eat. And together, we started something in our part of the country that wasn't altogether bad. But after a few years we discovered that we couldn't stop the stuff if we wanted to!

Actually, the kudzu plant came to the United States from Japan in 1876, when it was grown in the Japanese pavillion at the Philadelphia Centennial Exposition.

The Americans liked the Japanese plant and began to use it as a shade plant. It grew thickly and could provide shade from the sun easily. And it had lovely, sweet smelling flowers. Furthermore, it would grow in almost any kind of soil. By the early thirties, farmers were putting out kudzu in lots of places where they had been unable to grow anything else.

A farmer in Florida started selling cuttings from his kudzu crop in the mail, and the U.S. Post Office Department investigated him for mail fraud because they thought nothing could grow as fast as he advertised his kudzu could. But once they saw it in action they dropped the charges and apologized to the farmer!

Now, of course, kudzu not only covers a lot of poor land. It also covers telephone poles, barns, trees and even threatens slow-moving cows. Like it or not, kudzu is with us to stay!

Kicking Tires

Like most Americans, I have always been fascinated by automobiles. As far back as I can remember, I have always been excited along about the fall of the year when the new models start hitting the showrooms.

However, as I've grown older — while I still am fascinated by the new cars in the showrooms — I often find myself watching the people about as much as I am looking at the cars.

And I've noticed that some people still kick the tires of a car they're thinking seriously about buying. This always used to be the case. No one in his right senses would think about buying a car without first kicking the tires.

Why? Well, some tire experts think it all began back in the early 1900s when the "clincher" tire was used on cars. This tire was held tightly against the rim by clamps, and you kicked it·to see if it was properly fastened and inflated.

Tires in those days lasted about 50 miles, on the average. And even during the heyday of the Model T in the late twenties and early thirties, a motorist could count on having a flat every few miles.

Tires were not only less durable in those days, but there were no paved roads such as we have today. The roads were full of bad bumps and holes, not to mention sharp rocks and jagged roots which would punch a hole in a tire every time they were hit.

In those days, 15 miles an hour was about as fast as anybody drove, and even that was a reckless speed on most roads!

Now, with our fast speeds, heavy cars and long hours of sustained driving, many tires are guaranteed for 40,000 or more miles.

So, if you want to be technical about it, kicking the tires doesn't really make much sense, I guess.

However, I have a different theory about why folks used to kick the tires before they bought a car. In those days, more people were accustomed to buying horses and mules than they were cars, and nobody would think of buying a horse or mule without carefully examining the animal's feet to see if they were sound. Since the tires were the car's "feet," it just came naturally to examine them before buying a car.

Oh, well. Maybe there are some new reasons for kicking tires in these modern times. Maybe it's more frustration than anything else, considering the price tags on the new flivvers.

Come to think of it, I think the last fellow I saw kick a tire did so right after he'd looked at the price sticker on the window!

Playthings

When I was a boy back during the Depression days, kids had very few bought playthings. Even at Christmas, we were lucky to get a sponge rubber ball, a sack of marbles, a box of jacks or, (for the girls), a dime store doll. As things got better, perhaps a bicycle.

There was no such thing as plastics, or electronics. Nothing that ran on batteries. And — to be sure — nothing like the space age toys of today's generation.

But, like kids of every generation, we had playthings all right. We invented and devised and rigged our own. We made slingshots and string baseballs. We salvaged old worn-out automobile tires and wagon wheel rims and barrel hoops for basketball goals.

We had our own miniature race tracks down steep hillsides, dashing recklessly down the slopes on our homemade version of skateboards, scooters and racing cars.

I have spent many happy hours rolling a steel hoop off an old wagon wheel hub, guiding it with a long piece of stiff wire with a u-shaped crook in one end. This was called a click and wheel, because it made a clicking sound as the hoop rubbed against the wire.

Another plaything we had was our homemade flying jenny. It was a massive two-by-12 inch board with a hole bored in the exact center, free-mounted on the top of a smooth stump or a heavy timber anchored in the ground, so that the board could turn round and round. With one person sitting out on each end of the board, another person would push it around and around at high speeds.

Some of us played a gamed called "peg." The equipment consisted of a "peg" which was a small piece of wood about like a fat cigar, and a broom handle. One would flip the "peg" into the air and swing at it as if hitting a baseball with a bat. Fielders in front of the hitter would try to catch the "peg" and toss it back and try to hit the stick, which by then had been laid down by the batter inside a circle where he had stood to hit it.

Another favorite game of boys who had pocket knives was mumblety-peg. This was played by flipping an open jackknife into the air and causing it to stick in the ground in various ways. Interestingly enough, this game got its name because the loser originally was required to draw a peg out of the ground with his teeth.

Such a simple thing as an old empty tin can was often converted into a good plaything, too. I've walked many a mile down a country road kicking a tin can in front of me as I walked. Some city kids, where they had pavement, were fortunate enough to get roller skates for Christmas. They would often play hockey with a can as the puck and broom handles as the sticks. But where I lived there was no such thing as pavement, and I never had a pair of roller skates.

I could name some golfers I know who started playing the game on "greens" which were places in a farm pasture fenced off with barbed wire to keep the cows off of them. Their golf ball was made of string, and their golf clubs were sassafras limbs with a crooked root on the bottom.

Maybe it's hard for youngsters of today to imagine that playing with such things could be fun. But I'd guess we got more real genuine pleasure out of our homemade play pretties than many of today's boys and girls do with their fancy expensive toys.

183

Playing Marbles

One of my favorite boyhood games back in the good ole days was marbles.

For many years it seemed that shooting marbles had just about passed into antiquity. I'd go for years without seeing any kids playing this simple game.

But in recent years it's making a big comeback, as a new generation is re-discovering the fun of shooting these little colorful glass balls.

Every summer they hold the three-day National Marbles Tournament, with boys and girls from states all over the country competing.

This game was once played by George Washington, Thomas Jefferson, John Quincy Adams, and other prominent Americans. It is still the favorite sport of an estimated 3 million youngsters in this country.

While some kids are whacking away at baseballs, golf balls or tennis balls, these youngsters are hunkered down on the ground with their aggies, glassies, cats eyes and sticks. And they don't take losing lightly, either!

Even though they might not be playing for keeps, they're today's sharp-eyed and accurate-thumbed marble shooters. And some of them may even be better at it than some of my boyhood buddies who used to beat me nearly every Sunday afternoon in our weekly marble slugfest.

When I was growing up, marbles was played as a sport by grown men as well as young boys and girls. In fact, just about every community in those days had its renowned marbles champion.

Actually, marbles is one of our oldest games, dating back to ancient times. It was introduced to America by British settlers.

Marbles flourished in the Depression and throughout the 1930s and 1940s, primarily because of the low cost of playing the game. But after World War Two, it just sort of languished away. The game was revived in 1976, when the Bicentennial re-awakened Americans' interest in their past.

A few years ago the Cub Scouts of America included marbles among its activities for earning merit badges and published a handbook on the game.

There are several marbles manufacturers left in this country, and their business is booming. I read recently that one of these companies annually rolls out 365 million marbles, half of which are used for playing. The rest are used for floral decorations and industrial purposes.

I'm glad marbles is making a big comeback. It's barrels of fun!

Cow Pasture Baseball

A well-known commercial refers to baseball, hot dogs and apple pie as some of the favorite things of the American people. I like all those things myself.

But baseball, as it is played today, is quite different from the way we country boys used to play it back in the good ole days.

Oh, the game itself is the same, but the equipment and surroundings are not. Why, I was about grown before I ever played baseball any place except in a cow pasture.

Every community had at least one pasture spot that was fairly level and which had a clearing big enough for a baseball field. So that became a favorite gathering place for us country boys on Saturday and Sunday afternoons for our baseball games.

We didn't have much if any bought equipment. There wasn't money to buy equipment, so we made our own. We made string balls, starting with a smooth round rock and winding string around it tightly until we got it the size of a baseball.

Our bats were fashioned from sturdy hickory limbs of the proper size and length. And our gloves were homemade work gloves, with some padding inserted to keep the ball from blistering our hands when we caught a hard one.

I'll never forget the hissing sound of that string ball as it was hurled toward the plate by some old country boy with an arm that was strong as an ox from wrestling with a plow all week.

There was lots of excitement in those cow pasture baseball games, which were always full of surprises, for both players and spectators.

Of course, there are some obvious hazards which come from playing baseball in a cow pasture, such as sliding into what you thought was second base, only to discover too late that it was something else!

City boys called their community ball parks sand lots. And though they were nothing to compare with today's youth baseball fields, they were a right smart better equipped than our cow pasture parks were.

Frequently, in those days, country boys would get up a game with their counterparts in town, and it would generally be quite a game! What the country boys lacked in finesse, they usually made up for in agility, brute strength and stamina.

And out of those cow pastures came a lot of players who went on to become legends in the great American game of baseball. And lots of us who didn't.

Outdoor Basketball

There are several things that I like about the game of basketball — now that I've gotten older — from a spectator's standpoint.

One is that it is a fast-moving game where there is seldom a dull moment and never a break in the action. But one of the main things I like about it is that it is played indoors and can be enjoyed in relative comfort, no matter what the weather may be like.

Seated in a modern, heated, well-lighted gymnasium watching a basketball game recently, I got to thinking how facilities for this fine sport have improved since the days when I grew up.

Basketball in those days for us was an outdoor sport, and it was not an unusual thing for basketball games to be called off because of rain. We did not have a gymnasium at that time, and our basketball court was a smoothed-off spot near the football field, completely out in the open. There were no lights, and so all the games were played in the daytime. On a cold day, it was a real bone-chilling event!

For the players themselves, the game of basketball in those days had handicaps that today's players would shudder to think about. Just imagine trying to dribble the ball along an uneven dirt court, which often got potholes in it as the season wore on. Sometimes, after a rain, we even had to dodge puddles of water on the court.

The basketball itself was an out-seam ball. In other words, the seams were on the outside rather than on the inside, as basketballs now are made, which meant that the seams were rough and uneven around the surface of the ball. That dictated some necessary deftness in ball handling.

Playing in the outdoors, wind was often a problem too. If you think a hard wind does tricks with a football, you should see what gusty winter winds will do to a big basketball on long outdoor shots!

Basketball players today sometimes complain about the eccentricities of the different gymnasiums they have to play in and of different basketball floors. Just imagine how much "variety" there was in those days of outdoor basketball courts, with their limed boundary lines, unlevel playing surfaces, and even backboards and baskets of uncertain dimensions.

But basketball was still a great game, even in those days. And for us country boys who were accustomed to playing with a basket hoop nailed to the side of a barn, such an arrangement as I have described was sophistication plus!

Next time you go to see a basketball game in one of our fine gymnasiums, sitting in temperature-controlled comfort and watching the action take place on a shiny hardwood or bright composition court, just think of how we used to play and watch the game back in the good ole days.

It will give you a renewed appreciation for modern sports!

Whistling

The other day I noticed that a good friend and associate of mine was whistling while he worked.

It got my attention, I think, because such contented whistling which was a once-common sound is seldom heard around the workplace anymore.

What has happened to the whistlers? How long has it been since you have heard someone coming down the road warbling at full blast? Do you ever hear anyone doing a tuneless whistle while puttering around at some odd job?

Whistling seems to be fading from the American scene, and we are losing something I'm afraid. Nothing much has ever been invented to ease life's vexations better than to pucker up and cut loose with a good loud whistle.

The first effect is on the whistler himself. It is absolutely impossible to stay in a bad state of mind and whistle at the same time. Usually you whistle when you're feeling good. But try it some day when the world looks gloomy. It's amazing how it changes your outlook!

Then, there is the effect on the people who are listening. The whistler convinces everyone in hearing distance that things can't be too bad. It makes you believe that here's a person at ease with the world and ready to tackle his problems. Not that whistling will necessarily solve many problems, but it does seem to help one's general outlook.

This sets me to thinking about another thing which has disappeared from the American scene, and that's yodeling. Why even cowboy singers hardly ever yodel anymore!

I can remember that when I was a boy we had several men in our community who would serenade each other across the hills and hollows about daybreak every morning with their yodeling. Each man in the community had his own special "holler," which became his soundmark.

As they got out at the crack of dawn and walked to the barn to feed the stock, these contented farmers would rear back and turn loose their vocal cords with a lusty yodel or "holler" which would carry a mile or two through the quiet crisp air of early morning. One would cut loose first, then another would answer, and pretty soon the whole community was alive with the tuneful sounds.

I suppose city fellows, who did not have the wide open spaces like our hills and hollows to holler across, had their substitute for it by singing in the bathtub. That was out for us, because we didn't have a bathtub.

At any rate, I'm for reviving the good ole American custom of whistling. Some of it might not be too tuneful or pretty, but it sure would beat a lot of today's so-called music by a country mile!

Phonographs

One of the most amazing gadgets of our modern age is the phonograph, today commonly called the record player.

Record players are so inexpensive and commonplace today that it seems strange to realize that they were a rare and expensive novelty as recently as 60 years ago.

I can still remember the big "Victrola" which was a prominent fixture in the "Big House" which was our living room and bedroom combined. Victrola was a common brand name for phonographs in those days, and everybody called phonographs "Victrolas," no matter what kind they were. Just as they called all refrigerators "Frigidaires."

Anyhow, our "Victrola" was in a big walnut cabinet, with a lid which was raised to give access to the turntable and the record compartment. A crank extended from one end, and it had to be "wound up" before a record could be played.

All the records were made of a brittle wax substance, and they broke into smithereenes if dropped. The tone arm was a short stubby handle, and the playing head was a heavy metal device about three inches in diameter. It pivoted up and down, and had a sharp steel needle which was inserted in the bottom.

The sound was quite tinny and distorted by today's standards, but it was great to us then. We could sit for hours and enjoy the music of various bands, or laugh at the quips of such comedians as The Three Aces or Amos 'n Andy.

I can remember my daddy telling about what a hard time he had believing that the phonograph really worked. The first time he saw and heard one, he suspected that somehow there was a man hidden inside that thing making all those sounds!

Of course, the "Victrola" that we had when I was growing up was quite an advanced machine, compared with earlier models.

The first ones I can remember were the old Edison machines which played cylindrically shaped records instead of flat discs.

These were very refined compared with the first models introduced by inventor Thomas A. Edison, who patented the phonograph on Feb. 19, 1878.

Up until after World War Two, all phonograph records were recorded at a speed of 78 revolutions per minute. In fact, it was not until 1948 that long-playing records like we have today were introduced. And the high fidelity and stereo recordings that we enjoy today are developments of more recent times, not to mention tape recorders, lasers, compact discs and other space age developments in the recording field. In fact, computers can now duplicate the sound of an entire symphony orchestra with a single technician at the controls.

We sort of take it all for granted nowdays. But we sure didn't in my growing-up days, when the big "Victrola" was a center of attention in every home that could afford one, and a fireside entertainment center in most households.

Five And Dime Stores

Remember the 5 and 10 cent stores? Probably not, unless you're past 40. At least, the kind we used to have back in the good ole days, when they were so much a part of our lives. Now they're all but gone, and mostly forgotten.

When I was growing up, the main place to shop in town was the dime store, as we called it. In fact, most families did the bulk of their shopping there, except for groceries.

Every town of several hundred or more population had at least one 5 and 10. In the big cities there were always several of them, usually custered together on the same street or on all four corners of an intersection in the main part of the city.

There were several nationally prominent dime store chains, each with hundreds of stores around the country. Every region had its smaller chains of dime stores. And in small country towns there were a lot of locally owned 5 and 10s.

Originally, they were so named because just about everything they sold could be bought for a penny, a nickel or a dime. Of course, there were some things that cost more, like major clothing items. But probably 75 percent of their items sold for a dime or less.

For a dime you could buy a pocket knife or a screwdriver, a pound of candy, rubber dolls that whistled or squealed when squeezed, bright colored sponge rubber balls or a huge sack of glass marbles.

Many things cost a nickel. Like a giant bag of fresh-popped popcorn. The popcorn popper was always stationed near the front entrance, so that its tantalizing aroma grabbed you the moment you entered the store, or even drew you inside from the sidewalk in front of the store.

There were numerous things to fascinate every member of the family. And on those rare occasions when we all got to go to town, we'd spend several hours in the 5 and 10 cent stores, mostly looking and wishing.

Mama would disappear in the piece goods and pattern department. Daddy headed for the hardware section. And we kids checked out the toys, candies and nuts. Santa Claus could handle his gift list for the entire family with a $5 bill.

Those were the days before do-it-yourself shopping. A clerk would follow you around and stand by to help you make each purchase. The clerks were mostly women and teenage girls, always dressed as neatly as if they were on their way to church. Many youngsters got their first job working at a dime store.

Now the 5 and 10s have fallen victim to "progress." As has the possibility of buying much of anything for a nickel or a dime.

But I reckon it's just as well that they're gone. Somehow, the idea of calling a store "the 75 cents and $1.50 store" just doesn't have an enticing ring to it!

Christmas Decorations

Maybe it's just the kid in me. But I still look forward to the Christmas season almost as much as I used to when I was growing up. The main difference is that Christmas seems to get here a lot quicker than it did when I was a few decades younger.

One of the things that makes Christmas so enjoyable is all of the special holiday decorations. And back in the good ole days, planning and making our own holiday decorations was one of the special joys of this season of the year.

We would start weeks ahead of time thinking up ways to make our homes and school rooms pretty and festive for the holiday season. Times were hard and money was scarce, and we never thought of such a thing as buying Christmas decorations, unless it was a little colored paper to wrap presents in.

I grew up out in the country, where we didn't have to buy a Christmas tree. We just went to the woods and cut down a choice little cedar or pine and hauled it home in a wagon. That was another part of the fun for us kids —picking out the tree we wanted, weeks or months ahead of time, and looking forward to decorating it at Christmas time.

One of the favorite decorations for the tree was long ropes of popcorn, with the individual kernels strung on a piece of heavy thread. Another tree decoration was made by coloring strips of paper with red and green wax crayons, pasting them together like links in a chain and draping this around the tree. We saved our tinfoil chewing gum wrappers all year so we could cut them into slender strips for icicles.

197

But I think the most beautiful decorations of all were made from sweetgum balls that we picked up from under the trees on our farm. We would carefully select the biggest ones and those with the longest stems, then dip them in aluminum paint and hang them on the tree with thread.

As I think back on my childhood, growing up during the times of the Depression, I marvel at how my parents and those of my acquaintenances managed to provide any of those little "extras" for us at Christmas.

For us, Christmas meant no outpouring of expensive presents such as is common in these more affluent times. It usually meant some extra special things to eat, such as fresh oranges and big red apples, some giant sticks of peppermint candy, and maybe a sponge ball or some other simple plaything. But we made do with what we had, with a lot of improvising and imagination thrown in. And we had lots of fun!

Children have a way of doing such things, no matter what their circumstances may be. And, I suppose, that's one of the things that makes this season so special for children — of all ages!

Rainy Days

"Rain, rain, go away! Come again some other day."
This little poetic saying, which most of us have heard recited all our lives, has never really expressed my sentiments about rain. I like rain!

There's no more delightful sound than rain falling on a tin roof. Unless it's the sound of crackling hickory wood in a fireplace on a cold winter night. These are sounds that I grew up with as a country boy, and I'll always cherish them.

Rainy days meant a respite from the fields and perhaps a little extra time to curl up with a favorite story book or the perennial wish book better known as the Sears Roebuck catalog.

If it was a Saturday or a summer day when school was not in session, it sometimes meant an afternoon with neighborhood boys with a homemade punching bag strung with bailing wire from a rafter in the barn hall.

But it also meant indoor chores, because my daddy always had plenty of work lined up to be done on rainy days, like shucking and shelling corn. Shop work was also another rainy day job for us on the farm.

When I was a young boy one of my jobs was to turn the crank on the bellows, which fanned the burning coal and kept it hot for the plow points to be sharpened with a big steel hammer on top of the anvil, while they were glowing red hot from the forge. There were many other repairs to be made on our equipment, too.

Long rainy winter nights were favorite times for our family around the big fireplace in the "Big House," which was our version of living rooms and bedrooms combined. Many times we would play games together, play the guitar and sing or just simply listen to my daddy tell stories — after all the homework for school was done.

Later on, after we became affluent enough to own a small battery-powered radio, we would hurry through the chores and with supper to turn on the radio and hear Amos 'n Andy, Lum 'n Abner, Fibber McGee and Molly and Henry Aldridge.

When the fire got low and bedtime came my daddy would reach up and get the big black family Bible, put on his wire-rimmed dime store glasses and read a chapter from God's Word.

Then we would all kneel down by our chairs and pray together, thanking God for the blessings of the day, asking His protection for the night and His guidance in the new day to come.

Quietly then we were off to our respective beds to snuggle down under a stack of warm quilts to fall asleep by the lullaby of rain on the tin roof. These are some of my favorite memories about the rainy days and nights of my boyhood.

For additional copies of "The Good Ole Days" send $8.95 plus $2.00 for postage and handling (total of $10.95 for each book ordered) to:

Mountaintop Press
P. O. Box 698
Albertville, Alabama 35950